"Verner debuts with an impas[sioned] [call for people to open] their doors and invite neighbors and strangers into their homes and lives. In an age when political leaders seek to build walls, she writes, it is necessary to reinforce the common, human bonds of community. Verner declares hospitality both a habit and a command, as it's a theme and practice found throughout the Bible. . . . Hospitality, she maintains, is not about 'Instagrammable' perfection but about displaying vulnerability and satisfying hunger for community. Helpful supplemental material includes discussion questions, a short reading list, and tips for practices of welcome. Verner's persuasive message to 'become a good neighbor' will appeal to Christians and general readers alike."

—PUBLISHERS WEEKLY

"Insightful, accessible, and engaging to its core, *Invited* is the nudge we need to fling open the door and let the crumbs fall where they may. Through vulnerable storytelling, Leslie Verner whittles the panic from our thoughts on hospitality, reminding us we've never been more equipped to connect than we are right now."

—SHANNAN MARTIN, author of *Falling Free* and *The Ministry of Ordinary Places*

"Hospitality is such a powerful space where we get to practice giving and receiving, entering into mutuality and communion. Leslie Verner has experienced this larger hospitality—a belonging to the larger human family. In the pages of *Invited*, she has brought some of that wisdom and goodness to us."

—IDELETTE MCVICKER, founder of *SheLoves*

"In *Invited*, Leslie Verner peels back the assumptions about what makes a good, safe, and hospitable life. . . . An invitation to move away from the isolating individualism of the American Dream and move toward a life full of community, no matter where we are planted."

—D. L. MAYFIELD, author of *The Myth of the American Dream*

"The exact message the church needs to hear today. Through personal narrative and compelling truth, Leslie Verner invites us into her story, stretching us to reevaluate the way we live and engage others in our own."

—**MICHELLE FERRIGNO WARREN**, author of *The Power of Proximity*

"Hospitality is far more than an open home. It is a way of life, the embodying of 'welcome' in relationships and across cultures. Leslie Verner's *Invited* is both an invitation to recognize our own hunger for community and a call to offer it to those around us. As you read, you'll be inspired to lean into deeper, ever more authentic hospitality."

—**RACHEL PIEH JONES**, author of *Stronger Than Death*

"I shudder at the word *hospitality* because it has been weaponized in Christian circles, especially for women. I wondered if *Invited* was another veiled shame message pointing out how I was failing yet again. It is not; instead, Leslie Verner breathes on the embers of connection we all long for, offering hope and examples of how you can invite others into your real life and forge life-giving relationships."

—**AMY YOUNG**, author of *Looming Transitions*

"'Love usurps fear in kingdom living,' Leslie Verner writes, and I grab my pen to star the line. As our world quakes with polarization, division, and loneliness, this—choosing love over fear—is how we begin to mend the fault lines. In warm, welcoming prose, *Invited* offers us a glimpse of God's unshakable kingdom, where all are welcome—and makes it a little easier for us to imagine becoming a part of it."

—**AMY PETERSON**, author of *Where Goodness Still Grows* and *Dangerous Territory*

Invited

Verner, Leslie,
Invited : the power of
hospitality in an age of
2019.
33305242998346
mi   08/02/19

Invited

The Power of Hospitality
in an Age of Loneliness

Leslie Verner

HERALD
P R E S S

Harrisonburg, Virginia

Herald Press
PO Box 866, Harrisonburg, Virginia 22803
www.HeraldPress.com

Library of Congress Cataloging-in-Publication Data
Names: Verner, Leslie, author.
Title: Invited : the power of hospitality in an age of loneliness / Leslie Verner.
Description: Harrisonburg : Herald Press, 2019. | Includes bibliographical
    references.
Identifiers: LCCN 2019008234| ISBN 9781513804835 (pbk. : alk. paper) |
    ISBN 9781513804842 (hardcover : alk. paper)
Subjects: LCSH: Hospitality—Religious aspects—Christianity.
Classification: LCC BV4647.H67 V47 2019 | DDC 241/.671—dc23
LC record available at https://lccn.loc.gov/2019008234

INVITED
© 2019 by Herald Press, Harrisonburg, Virginia 22803. 800-245-7894.
    All rights reserved.
Library of Congress Control Number: 2019008234
International Standard Book Number: 978-1-5138-0433-0 (paperback);
978-1-5138-0434-7 (hardcover); 978-1-5138-0435-4 (ebook)
Printed in United States of America
Cover and interior design by Merrill Miller
Cover image adapted from art by pridumala/Getty Images/iStockphoto

All rights reserved. This publication may not be reproduced, stored in a re-
trieval system, or transmitted in whole or in part, in any form, by any means,
electronic, mechanical, photocopying, recording or otherwise without prior
permission of the copyright owners.

    Unless otherwise noted, Scriptures are taken from the *Holy Bible, New
International Version*®, NIV®. Copyright © 1973, 1978, 1984, 2011 by Biblica,
Inc.™ Used by permission of Zondervan. All rights reserved worldwide. www
.zondervan.com The "NIV" and "New International Version" are trademarks
registered in the United States Patent and Trademark Office by Biblica, Inc.™
    Scripture taken from *The Message*. Copyright © 1993, 1994, 1995, 1996,
2000, 2001, 2002. Used by permission of NavPress Publishing Group.
    Scripture taken from *New Revised Standard Version Bible*, copyright
© 1989, Division of Christian Education of the National Council of the
Churches of Christ in the United States of America. Used by permission.
All rights reserved.

23 22 21 20 19   10 9 8 7 6 5 4 3 2 1

To Elijah, Adeline, and Isaiah, my littlest guests.
And to Adam, my home.

CONTENTS

Author's Note

People say hospitality is about making guests feel at home, but most of what I know about hospitality I learned as a stranger far from home. Many cultures of the world have an intrinsic understanding of hospitality unfamiliar to those of us from countries typically considered to be in "the West." My conclusions for this book arose out of my graduate studies, traveling and living abroad, and having international students live with my family in the United States.

Instead of a didactic "how to" book, *Invited* offers stories that reframe and perhaps even redefine hospitality. Less about entertaining and more about becoming a good neighbor, this book explores the power of a simple invitation.

My goal in writing this is to delve deeper—in relationship with God and the people around us, in understanding our resistance to hosting and being hosted, and in grasping courage to cultivate community wherever we are in the world.

I changed the names of most of the people in this book out of respect for their privacy. Also, because of the book's nature as partial memoir, I reconstructed dialogue, descriptions, and events as accurately as I remember them or as recorded in my journals. Some parts of these stories previously appeared on my own blog, *Scraping Raisins*, or as articles for *SheLoves Magazine*.

When I use a phrase like "we in the West" or speak of "Western" culture, I'm primarily referring to white people who have some heritage or association with Europe and whose majority culture is of European descent. And yet "Western" assumptions are not limited to white people but also include people of many racial and ethnic backgrounds who live in Western countries. Living in a place influences our behavior, thoughts, and daily practices, so anyone who has lived for any period of time in a Western country is effectively influenced by "Western" thought. I know that living in China poured a tiny bit of "Eastern" culture into me.

—*Leslie Verner*

I am the one whose love
overcomes you, already with you
when you think to call my name . . .

—Jane Kenyon

Introduction

Hospitality for our family usually looks like this: I wait until the last minute to tell my children we're having guests, because they morph into crazed creatures pulsating with energy the second they know more attention-giving bodies will be in our home. When my pre-arrival stress threatens to erupt, I turn on a movie for the kids as I sweep up crumbs and issue marching orders to my husband-turned-servant. Seconds before our first guest arrives, we scan the house, noting the value of having guests even if it's just to have a decluttered home. But then the reality check arrives.

The doorbell rings and my two boys hide, while my daughter rushes to the door, suddenly all disheveled hair and stained clothing, and drags any kid guests to her and her brother's messy bedroom. The guests make their way to the kitchen and plant themselves at the kitchen island. My husband, Adam, delivers drinks while I try not to screw up the whole meal in minutes because I'm now not only stressed and hungry but distracted. The kids dash through the house, dumping dolls from baskets and crashing trucks over our feet. They reach grimy hands over the counter to blindly grab at olives, cheese, or chips.

I calmly and slowly remind my children of What We Talked About Before Our Guests Arrived: they should play outside or in designated rooms. Go there right now. *Please.* They ignore me. I stand there, fingers covered in garlic, knife in hand, and keep smiling at my newly arrived guests.

Welcome to our happy home.

Once we invited our friends Dave and Amy over with their three kids the same ages as our kids, and one man, Pete, who came solo. Adam and I spent the entire afternoon preparing. The shrimp, potatoes, and corn were overcooked and too salty, and I learned the downside of the popular "open floor plan"— namely, that child chaos ricochets around the room and messes are impossible to conceal behind closed doors. The four older children (all five and under) sat alone at the kitchen island, dueling with plastic knives they snuck out of the drawer and turning their bread into ships and guns. The kids finished and Dave and Amy's three-year-old daughter, Cate, smashed her finger in the sliding glass door and wailed the remainder of the time. We all stood up, leaving Pete to eat his apple pie alone at the table.

When our friends' baby began to shriek, the parents abruptly announced their decision to abort mission, and Pete decided to leave too. What was meant to last two and a half hours lasted one. Within minutes, Adam and I stood in the aftermath of counters piled high with dirty dishes as our overstimulated kids sprinted across the toy- and food-littered floor.

"Let's go for a walk," I said.

I dropped back and sauntered alone while Adam pushed the stroller in front of me and the older two kids raced ahead on the sidewalk. In the quiet after the pandemonium, I did what any halfway sensible adult would do: I reflected on the wisdom of continuing the stress, anxiety, and humiliation of having people over to my home. Maybe this isn't the time of life. Perhaps I just say I like hospitality because it seems like the Good Christian Thing to say. God, is this really . . . ?

And before I could even formulate the thought into a prayer, God seemed to interrupt my thoughts with these words:

You do it anyway.

Wait, what?

You do hospitality anyway, God seemed to say. *You do it in the stress and the mess and the raisins smashed into the carpet. You do it when you're hollering over three preschoolers telling knock-knock jokes with no punchline and talking about poop and pee at the table. You do it when your children throw tantrums and blatantly disobey you in front of your friends and family. You do it because doing life together means not hiding behind closed doors but inviting people into your actual life. And your actual life is not pretty. It's not organized, perfect, or pristine.*

You do it because I am a hospitable, generous God and because Jesus was a model of serving despite inconveniences. You invite because I invited you, and you welcome because the Bible says you may well bring angels in disguise into your home.

And you invite because when you invite, you are inviting me.

A cloth is not woven from
a single thread.

—Chinese proverb

ONE

The Quest for Community

tangle of tumbleweed skittered across Interstate 80 as we drove west through the bleak plains of Nebraska. So appropriate, I thought, gripping the steering wheel and weaving to avoid the cartwheeling, rootless branches blowing far from their origin. So much like us. Adam, the kids, and I were on our way back to Colorado after a short visit to Chicago, and I held back tears as we left what still felt like home for a place where we were friendless and unknown.

Although Chicago had nurtured me through early adulthood as I shared an apartment with friends for four years after college, its abusive Januaries had punctured my soul, and it felt as if more of me seeped out with each winter. When I left the city to live in northwest China for five years, I never missed the way the sun hid behind a slate sheet of cloud for weeks on end, rarely emerging between November and May. When I returned to the States to marry Adam, my whispered fear of being trapped with an infant in a frigid Chicago apartment in the vortex of winter quickly materialized.

Chicago yanked the covers of seasonal affective disorder right up to my nose, choking my joy and darkening my demeanor. Parallel parking three blocks away, lugging one, then two children, strollers, and groceries through snow drifts up to our third-floor apartment eventually rusted our shiny resolve to never sell out to the suburbs. We couldn't afford to buy a home in the city anyway, so we began the conversation that culminated in a cross-country move to a place boasting three hundred days of sun a year.

We crossed the Colorado-Nebraska border as the amber sun burned in my rearview mirror. Our kids were little, so Adam and I preferred to make the fifteen-hour drive at night to stopping every hour during the day. The kids still slept, somehow comfortably crooked in their car seats. The Rocky Mountains in the distance were pink in the fresh sunlight, and black cows scattered across the grasslands on either side of the highway. I thought about how, in moving from Chicago to northern Colorado, we had unknowingly stepped into a foreign culture. At first glance, Colorado is a mix of handguns and pickup trucks, marijuana dispensaries and craft beer spots, hiking trails and shops called One Love and the Hazy Hippo. Suburban homes are zoned for chicken coops, and even large cities have horses penned behind gas stations and strip malls. Mountains peek out from behind Target, and the smell of manure from nearby cattle ranches wafts through parking lots. Rocks carpet the lawns, rattlesnakes nestle in the grass, and clothes dry stiff on the line within an hour. Women follow folklore and wind up the mountains to induce labor by the altitude. Churches like God's Country Cowboy Church have mini rodeo rinks in the church parking lot.

We've been in Colorado for more than three years, yet I still feel like a foreigner here. I'm told that the wide roads in our city of Fort Collins, just fifty minutes south of Cheyenne, left room for pioneer wagons to turn around with horses when the land was settled by white people, who forced Native Americans in the area onto reservations in 1878. Colorado still has the air of frontier independence, the whiff of the first European settlers who abandoned the familiar to prove they could handle life well enough on their own.

But despite cerulean skies, sun that warms your skin even in January, and mountain peaks that flaunt their beauty, Colorado still has one of the highest suicide rates in the country.[1] Loneliness laces its fingers around even the most physically fit, ecologically conscious, and financially secure, sometimes tightening its noose-like grip to the point of fatal despair.

According to the American Psychological Association, loneliness is an epidemic not only in particular states but in the United States in general.[2] About one-third of U.S. adults age forty-five and older report feeling lonely. The top predictors of loneliness are the "size and diversity of an individual's social network and being physically isolated."[3] The problem is not unique to the United States. The United Kingdom even hired a "minister of loneliness" to help combat their loneliness problem.[4] Psychologist Susan Pinker reports that in the United States "more than sixty-two million people . . . say they are socially isolated and unhappy about it. More than half of them (thirty-two million) live alone."[5]

Churchgoers are not immune to the grip of loneliness. A quick Google search of "lonely at church" yields hundreds of articles. Sunday mornings can feel like the loneliest time of the week when we expect soul connection and experience only weak coffee and shallow small talk. Or worse, no talk at all.

We visited our tenth church in Colorado a few months before I gave birth to our third child. We never set out to be church hoppers, but somehow our family of four, and eventually five, visited eighteen churches in the first three years we lived in Colorado.

"You can choose how you want to worship," a man had announced from the front of that tenth church. "Take communion at the back right corner, write down prayer requests and hang them on the cross, come forward for prayer, or remain in your seat to pray or sing."

We had attended two different churches for nearly a year, leaving each because of differences in priority and theology. In all the churches we visited, we hadn't been just lackadaisical visitors, attending without effort to introduce ourselves to new people. We had joined small groups, potlucks, parties, and outreaches. We went to retreats, newcomers' luncheons, Sunday school, and women's ministry events. But climbing into our car after church, we had still felt like land detached from its rightful continent, drifting beyond the shore.

At this tenth church, a man on stage plucked strings on his guitar and a woman sang softly into the microphone, "Here I am to worship, here I am to bow down, here I am to say that you're my God," the words projected onto giant screens on either side of the stage.

I started singing, then sensed the silence of the people around us. I glanced over my shoulder at the back corner to see a round table displaying a tray of plastic cups and a plate of wafers. A middle-aged woman approached the table alone, tipped the tiny cup to her lips, flicked the wafer onto her tongue, and returned to her seat. A man stepped up to the stage after the time of worship ended and preached for thirty minutes, a digital clock on the side of the wall ticking backward to show the time remaining in his sermon.

When the service ended, people chatted in pairs. No one approached us, spoke to us, shook our hands, or asked us a question. A woman sitting just a few chairs away darted out without making eye contact. I sat next to Adam, hand propped on my pregnant belly, tears streaming down my face.

* * *

As I consider this church experience, I wonder if some churches are being held captive by our individualistic Western culture. In the sea of a grand Christian theology that beckons us to die to ourselves, live for others, and welcome strangers, individualism is the silent, lethal undertow luring the North American church away from the shore of genuine community. We often don't realize we're caught in the flow, much less know how to swim against the stream.

I didn't even realize I had a culture until I lived with a Ugandan family for six months during my senior year of college. Like air, breathing, economic security, and health, I took my culture for granted until I was no longer surrounded by it. Away from my Western culture, I gasped for breath, astounded that every rule I had considered to be universal had shifted. Body language, vocabulary, attitude, daily rituals, social expectations, and even what was considered "biblical" all carried mysterious underlying assumptions that I scrambled to decode. I felt as if I were walking on the ceiling and lying down on the walls.

Professor Soong-Chan Rah notes in *The Next Evangelicalism* that "the cultural captivity of the church has meant that the church is more likely to reflect the individualism of Western philosophy than the value of community found in Scripture."[6] When we construct our sermons, services, small groups, songs, and Bible studies to focus on "me" and "I" instead of the communal church or God, we allow our culture to inform our churches instead of the other way around.[7]

Individualism has led us offshore, leaving us wondering how we can get back to where we started—back to the promises of Eden and God strolling with a couple in the garden. Back to being loved even though we are strangers. Back to belonging in a community of people who love us unconditionally.

* * *

One evening after moving to Colorado, I escaped the house at dusk to roam the silent streets of our neighborhood, pretending not to gaze into the glowing windowpanes of the apartments and homes. I paused under the streetlight at a Little Free Library, a box set up for neighbors to swap free books. I took my hands out of my pockets to shuffle through the random titles and found a slim, unfamiliar volume on American culture, a book called *The Pursuit of Loneliness*.

During the kids' naptime the next day, I flipped through and discovered it was originally written in 1970 by a sociologist named Philip Slater. Published at a time before our smartphones could be consulted about where to eat a meal, for directions, or about what to do about bullies at school, Slater's words were prophetic. He suggested that our deep needs for community, engagement, and dependency "are suppressed in our society out of a commitment to individualism."[8] From the time we're babies sent to sleep alone in other rooms, we're molded for independence. He wrote,

> We seek a private house, a private means of transportation, a private garden, a private laundry, self-service stores, do-it-yourself skills of every kind. An enormous technology seems to have set itself the task of making it unnecessary for one human being ever to ask anything of another in the course of going about his or her daily business. Even within the family Americans are unique in their feeling that each member should have a separate room and even a separate telephone, television, and car, when economically possible. We seek more and more privacy, and feel more and more alienated and lonely when we get it.[9]

I wondered if the author knew that Jesus carried the discussion so much further. Rather than living for self, Jesus and his followers forfeited personal comfort for the sake of selfless love. "Practice hospitality," Paul urged the Roman church. "Share with [God's] people who are in need," he says, and then echoes the words of Jesus himself: "Bless those who persecute you; . . . rejoice with those who rejoice; mourn with those who mourn" (Romans 12:13-15). Privacy can be the enemy of the open home.

As Middle Easterners, Jesus and his followers dwelled within a culture that highly valued community, hospitality, and relationships. Hospitality was their default response to friends, guests, and strangers, not their extraordinary act of service. Community was built in, not sought out. But in the West, our default is privacy, individualism, and independence. The United States is listed as number one on the individualism index, a measure used by researchers to determine how where we live influences how we think about the role of the individual versus the role of the group. Australia ranks number two on the individualism index, with Great Britain and Canada as three and four. In contrast, most countries in South and Central America, Africa, and Asia fall much lower on the list, valuing the group over the individual. In fact, write the authors of one study, "collectivism is the rule in our world, and individualism the exception."[10] With such a high value on individualism and privacy, it's no wonder many of us in the West feel isolated and lonely.

* * *

Around our third anniversary of moving to Colorado, I remember tripping the blinker with my hand and easing the car out into traffic on our way to the grocery store. I had been thinking about something but wondered if I was correct. At a stoplight, I glanced back to catch my five-year-old son's eye. I asked, "Elijah, do you remember going to anyone's house for a meal since moving to Colorado?" I knew we had, but my calculations seemed ridiculously low. Could it be that we had been invited to someone's home just three times in three years?

"We went to Faraz and Sara's house," he said, not realizing I was counting churchgoers. Faraz and Sara were the three- and six-year-old children of our Iranian international student friends who had stayed with us five nights before moving to an apartment near campus. In fact, international students had invited us to eat Chinese hotpot, homemade pizzas, or spicy chicken stews in their apartments more times than North Americans from church had invited us over.

Perhaps it's intimidating to host a family with three small children. Or maybe busy schedules, finicky eaters, restrictive diets, dirty houses, stressful jobs, or cooking phobias prevented others from inviting us over. Perhaps the lack of invitations was because life just barrels on, and Western culture rarely demands that we invite one another into our perceived personal chaos. At least these are the things I told myself. Without those explanations, I'd begin to deduce that the subtle snub indicated people didn't like us.

A single meal does not community make, but it has the potential to remind us we're not solo wanderers in the wilderness. An invitation is a slight opening in the window of relationship, granting intimacy permission to drift in like a breeze into a stuffy room.

Hospitality, while still vibrant in some areas of the West, has mostly become a faded dream in a fast-paced society. Resurrecting this old-fashioned value has the power not only to satiate our personal loneliness, but also to enliven our faith communities, revitalize our neighborhoods, and transform our cities. The Bible clearly commands followers of God to welcome others, open our homes, and love our neighbors. "Offer hospitality to one another without grumbling," Peter urges the church in 1 Peter 4:9. Peter seems to use this as an answer to the previous verse: "Above all, love each other deeply, because love covers over a multitude of sins." Love errs on the side of invitation.

Hospitality is the marrow of community, the life source that produces the very cells our collective humanity needs to function.

But what does God *really* expect when the Bible commands us to "show hospitality"? That we invite our neighbors for dinner every night? Convert our minivans into shuttles for people who are homeless, bringing strangers home to eat casseroles with our families? How far does God want us to go when it comes to loving our neighbor? And how much does our culture muddle the clarity of God's commands?

* * *

Living in China for five years as an adult offered me plenty of snapshots of communal living. As a twenty-six-year-old, I had quit my job teaching seventh grade in Chicago, sold my car, and moved to China to teach English to college students. My first three years I lived in a small city unknown even to most Chinese people I met when traveling to other provinces. A man from Hong Kong once compared my city to the China of sixty or maybe even one hundred years ago. The president of our university was the only staff member who owned a private car, and taxi fare was forty cents to travel anywhere in the city. The nearest airport was an eight-hour drive until a highway opened up a few months after my arrival, halving the travel time. We were, by anyone's standards, "remote."

On one of my trips to the countryside to visit the family of one of my students, her mother had invited three friends to teach us to dance. As a single woman living alone, I couldn't remember the last time I had ballroom danced, much less with a middle-aged woman as my partner. The Chinese farmer's sandpaper palms chafed my smooth ones as we waltzed on the cold brick of the living room floor, odors of garlic, earth, and burnt charcoal surrounding us. She grinned, just inches from my face, and we mimicked dancers on television who twirled and spun in evening gowns on the screen while ballroom music blasted from dusty speakers into the room.

In winter, these goji berry farmers often congregated in each other's homes, playing cards or switching on the dance channel before harvest called them out to pluck tiny red berries from waist-high bushes. Although I knew life as a farmer was harsh and monotonous, I envied their community, the way they danced away the wicked winter months. I had rarely experienced this type of community, brought on by the simple hospitality of an open invitation to congregate, celebrate, and enjoy each other's presence.

Living and traveling in countries like Uganda, China, Thailand, Laos, Tajikistan, and Kenya, I noted the implications of favoring life together over life alone. There were certainly downsides, but I also wondered what I could learn from their strengths.

* * *

A Chicago native once told me he thought of Chicago as a city of small towns, like a patchwork quilt. Each separate neighborhood on the north side of the city has its own downtown area with unique eateries, coffee shops, and local treasures. With thousands of people living on every city block, sharing buildings, playgrounds, restaurants, and transportation, Chicago had seemed like the perfect setup for communal living. But cities are like fish tanks stocked with exotic fish waiting to be bought and transferred to their new home. The ever-shifting ground makes it a risky landscape for putting down permanent roots.

The people who do make Chicago their forever home abide by the unspoken code of conduct for urban dwellers: although you hear your neighbor yell at his kid, make love to his wife, mash his shrieking alarm clock, and flush his toilet, you pretend you don't. Somehow, city dwellers maintain a sense of privacy and autonomy even in the midst of a crowd. In my nine years of living in the city, I resisted the urge to peer into apartment windows even though they were a glimpse into another life. And I learned that living communally does not guarantee community.

Two years after leaving China and the year before I had my first child, I taught fourth grade at a small private school in Chicago's Chinatown. I commuted on the Red Line of Chicago's rail system, called the L, for fifty minutes each way.

One morning I gathered my hat, gloves, and backpack as train after train barreled through the station across the street. As a train whizzed by, its windows reflected rare sunbeams back into our condo in staccato bursts of magenta, violet, and gold. I wished I could entrap them for another dreary day.

I zipped my coat, wiggled my fingers into mittens, and hurried out the door and across the street. Ascending the stairs, I hovered under the orange glow of the heat lamp on the platform until the train swept in to swallow me up with all the other commuting strangers. Train passengers wore headphones, read books, or scrolled through pictures, news, or books on their phones. I had moved to China in 2005, at the height of the flip phone era, but when I returned to Chicago in 2010, everything had changed.

As the L rumbled and stopped, rumbled and stopped, I thought about how classrooms now had access to laptops, iPads, and iPods, and how more people than not carried a computer in their pocket. As a teacher, I was now expected by parents and school administrators to be on call at all hours. Every homework and test grade I recorded electronically was instantly available online.

For better or worse, the smartphone had significantly altered how we work, communicate, and experience life together.

In an article about the effects of smartphones on teenagers, Jean Twenge notes that "rates of teen depression and suicide have sky-rocketed since 2011." She claims that "it's not an exaggeration to describe iGen as being on the brink of the worst mental-health crisis in decades. Much of this deterioration can be traced to their phones."[11]

The first iPhone was released in 2007 while I was living in China, but Twenge notes that a huge shift occurred in 2012, when the number of Americans who owned a smartphone tipped past 50 percent. According to her research, this was when teens began to sleep less, feel lonelier, detach from friend groups, date and go out less, and have higher suicide rates.

Glancing out the L window at the gray skies and blinking buildings, I thought about how our phones tug at the threads of community, intimacy, and relationship. Would they lead to our unraveling, or be another strand that would strengthen the fabric of our existence? Much of what we used to ask a human, we now inquire of Google. We used to seek advice from friends, mothers, sisters, and grandmothers about feeding, bathing, clothing, and sleeping our little ones. Now, we punch questions into search bars or ask two thousand strangers in a Facebook group. Convenience whisks us out of relationship as we no longer need to grocery shop, talk on the phone, or enter a store where we might interact with another human being. We dive into our portals to the virtual world rather than relate to the souls standing, sitting, or sniffling next to us. And yet we marvel that we're so lonely.

An icy gale blew through the open doors as we stalled at the Wilson stop. Wilson Avenue stretches through a neighborhood called Uptown, home to halfway houses and wig shops, homeless shelters, hole-in-the-wall eateries, and a jazz club called the Green Mill that birthed the poetry slam and was once a hangout for Al Capone. Wilson Avenue was not only the first street where I had lived in Chicago but also home to the first intentional community I visited.

As a junior in college, I had ventured from the Chicago suburbs, where my college was located, into Uptown to do research for a sociology class. The intentional Christian community called Jesus People USA (JPUSA) was on Wilson Avenue, just a few blocks from the L. At the time, I was in awe of the shaggy dreadlocks, bones in noses, gaping holes in ear lobes, and tattoos peeking out of sleeves and pant legs. I joined church members for a buffet lunch in the cafeteria after the church service, and a family invited me up to their room in the Friendly Towers, the renovated hotel where the community members lived.

We sat at their kitchen table overlooking the bustling street below, sipping coffee and chatting. After a while, I began asking more intrusive questions. "So you share all your money?" I asked. Their preteen children, whose room was the next door over, poked their heads into the kitchen to say they were running downstairs to see a friend. "What about if you need clothes or shoes? Or if you want to buy an engagement ring to get married? Where do you work? Do you give your whole paycheck to JPUSA?" I asked, taking another sip of coffee. I had so many questions.

I had been enthralled with the unfamiliar cultural norms, the sharing, and the commitment to community at the expense of individual rights. Surely this was Christian community as God intended it to be? Some aspects reminded me of the parts of college life that I enjoyed—living on the same floor as my friends, eating meals together, and sharing common spaces—but I also wondered what was going unsaid. What goblins of conflict, control, or abuse lurked in the commune closets? Surely life couldn't be as ideal as it seemed.

People in Christian communities—like JPUSA in Chicago, the Simple Way Community in Philadelphia, Rutba House in Durham, and hundreds of others—intentionally eat together, pray together, and embody a shared vision for developing relationships and serving their neighbors. But do followers of Jesus need to join an intentional community to cultivate true community?

I always believed God drew us the blueprint for life together in the Bible. Paul describes an idyllic, nearly eye-roll-inducing picture of community in Acts 2: shared bread, money and resources, prayer, worship, and common purpose. As a white American who grew up attending summer camps, when I read this passage I used to envision the disciples sitting cross-legged by candlelight singing "Kumbaya" to an acoustic guitar. Although I know it's not realistic, I still wish it could be our reality. Mostly, I long to know and be known.

Some North Americans do live communally without joining communes. Architect Grace Kim talks about copying the Danish idea of cohousing, in which families live in homes in close proximity to one another, sharing frequent meals in a community house. Kim suggests that cohousing can make us happier and live longer. She says that "instead of pursuing the American Dream where we might have been isolated in our single-family homes, we instead chose co-housing, so we can increase our social connections."[12]

Although most of us will never cohouse or join an intentional community, we may taste communal living at summer camps, retreats, or college dormitories. Graduate school families may send their children racing up and down the stairwell of their student housing complexes, borrowing sugar and bartering babysitting. When the three or five years end, they lament the loss of community, usually trading it for a single-family home in the suburbs.

The L rumbled past Graceland Cemetery, and I wondered about the people buried there. Had they found friendship and community, laughter and love? Was it easier "back then" to strike up a conversation with a stranger or forget busyness to linger over a shared meal?

The train eventually dipped into the bowels of the city's underground tunnels, and I pulled out a book to read until we crept back up into the daylight. In all my commutes, I rarely struck up conversations with the strangers I literally rubbed shoulders with on crowded rides home during rush hour. Exiting the train, I wound down the stairs and into Chinatown, with its ornate buildings and scarlet signs. Wentworth Avenue was lined with day laborers crouching on the sidewalk, smoking and waiting to be picked up to work in restaurants in the suburbs. Chinatown was its own kind of complicated community, with those of similar cultures and languages banding together in a single neighborhood.

After spending five years in China, I had hoped to trick myself into feeling as if I were living abroad again by choosing to work in a Chinatown school. What I didn't realize back then was that I'd eventually seek out other languages, cultures, ethnicities, and former expats in Colorado in an effort to find "home" in a place within my own country, which felt foreign and unfamiliar.

* * *

During our second year in Colorado, I discovered the International Women's Club, an informal meeting of university students and wives of doctoral and master's degree students from other countries. On Friday mornings we twisted newsprint into flowers to paint, learned how to make samosas, or mimicked the volunteer yoga instructor, bending our bodies into mountain and warrior poses as our little ones mirrored our moves.

I waved goodbye to the women after one of our meetings. Lina, from Indonesia, nursed her baby beneath the flap of her robe while she chatted with two Chinese women who were feeding blueberries to their toddlers.

"Can we play, can we play?" my three- and five-year-olds begged, tugging my pant leg.

"Yes, you can play," I answered, although they had already run out into the cool Colorado air. I tied my baby, Isaiah, onto my chest with a baby wrap, and he buried his head in my cotton shirt. Motel-like apartments for international students faced inward, guarding a grassy courtyard with sidewalks connecting the two buildings. A breeze traipsed in and out of open windows and doors, flinging stray golden leaves onto the screens, which acted like a sieve. I nodded to an Indian granny as she swept the sidewalk. Many residents lived with their mothers, who flew in from their home countries to cook meals, care for children, and handwash clothes.

The international student coordinator had taped invitations to each apartment door, alerting residents to a movie night at the rec center. Chinese couplets clung to the frames of some doors, the fragile paper peeling away at the corners. Bikes leaned against brick walls next to patches of dirt where some tenants grew mint, scallions, and tomatoes, which glistened orange on their stalks. Colorful saris snapped in the wind on clotheslines behind the building.

Catching up to my children, who were sliding, climbing, and hiding on the playground, I noticed additions to the colony of misfit toys over the summer. A faded pink plastic play kitchen, broken bikes, and even a child-sized easy chair had been donated or discarded by families before returning home to their countries.

"Hello!" a voice called behind me. I whirled to see my friend Ekta walking toward me. Her four-year-old son skipped up behind her, dashing to join my children at the play set. The three children traded shy hellos, but soon chased one another out of sight around the side of the building.

"Do you want to walk around the courtyard here?" she asked. Seeing me glance toward the kids, Ekta added, "The kids will be fine."

"Sure," I answered. A boy about Elijah's age with dark skin and black hair darted out, then an Asian girl in a floral dress joined them, the screen door slamming shut behind her.

"This is so great to have this playground here. And all these kids," I said. I thought of our new home, less than three miles away. The previous owners had installed a wooden play set with swings, a plastic slide, and even a small rock climbing wall in the backyard, but the kids hadn't been too keen on it, preferring to play at the neighborhood park down the street.

"Yeah, it's really wonderful," Ekta said. "The adults take turns watching the kids. It's nice to have an hour or two to yourself." I agreed, thinking of all the money I had spent on a babysitter that week.

Laughing, I said, "You know this isn't what the United States is *really* like, right?"

Did Ekta, who is from India, realize the contrast between her communal life and the isolation of her American neighbors down the street? From my perspective, she seemed to be experiencing the community I longed for in my own neighborhood, what I ached to find at church.

Her experience as a guest in the United States reminded me of the verse I had loved as a teenager and turned to in every transition, though I didn't quite grasp its context at the time: "'For I know the plans I have for you,' declares the Lord, 'plans to prosper you and not to harm you, plans to give you hope and a future'" (Jeremiah 29:11). Speaking to the Israelites in exile in another country, God had encouraged them to go ahead and marry, have children, plant gardens, and eat the shiny orange tomatoes. He urged them to build homes and purchase bikes for their children that they'd one day need to leave behind (see Jeremiah 29:5-7, my paraphrase).

God asked them to labor for the peace and prosperity of the foreign city where they lived and to pray for its welfare. This was not their permanent home, but they were to act like it was. Community started with a seed and a single root—wherever God's children planted themselves. And hospitality acted like water to barren ground.

A fig tree cannot walk,
but its roots go very far.

—Congolese proverb

TWO

Staying Put

ade for More," the poster in the church atrium announced in large, bold letters. Against a backdrop of
mountains, a woman with a nose ring gazed up with a slip of
a smile on her face. I paused in front of the advertisement for
the class on world missions, noting that it bothered me. I wondered why.

As a teenager and young adult, I had never dreamed of
showing hospitality to the people in my own front yard. I
planned to love strangers as far from home as possible. I never
wanted to own a home, either, or to have two hundred salad
dressing options at the grocery store, or to raise my children
speaking just one language. That was not The Plan.

When I was sixteen, I remember typing homework on our
desktop computer in my dad's office in our spare room. I had
just "answered the call" to the nations at a church missions
conference. My mom bent over her desk next to me, crunching

numbers for my dad's business, when I blurted out, "I don't think I'm going to live the white picket fence life, Mom." I knew I was destined for more than the middle-class future my parents had labored for me to have.

Soon after that, I waited in a movie theater before the film began with a group of other teenagers, our feet propped on the back of the seats in front of us. One of the girls from my church leaned forward and asked me, "Hey—so you really want to be a missionary?" She sat back in her seat. "I don't think I could do that. I mean, I'll go if God wants me to go, but I want to *stay*."

I paused before eating another fistful of popcorn and laughed, saying, "I feel just the opposite: I'll stay if God wants me to stay, but I want to *go*."

Fast-forward ten years, and the cyclone whisked me away to Oz, only to bring me back five years later to the Kansas (okay, Chicago) I hadn't yet learned to miss. Five years after that, it blew me even farther west, to the foothills of the Rocky Mountains, and eventually to a home in a neighborhood one minute from a mall, five minutes from Target, and so far from the radical life I had imagined for myself.

Somewhere along the way, I had internalized the church messages that placed missionaries at the top of the Loving-God Hierarchy, those in full-time ministry below that, and everyone else on the bottom rung. The North American church has a cult of calling that clothes those who leave "the ministry" for the marketplace with shame and guilt. For me, the message had always been clear: going was more holy than staying. Stayers were selling out; goers adventured with God. If you were "made for more," how could you settle for less?

Overall, the United States is a country of leavers, goers, and explorers. Admittedly, much of this wanderlust is often connected with the middle- and upper-class segments of the population who have the financial ability to pursue jobs and education in other cities. Our most densely populated areas are transient and ripple with the motion of newcomers and out-goers. The perpetual motion can leave us addicted to change, nervous when still, and wild with boredom when we finally buy a home and settle down. We soon begin to wonder "Where's next?"—and in some cases "Who's next?"

Many of us carry our Western culture of "going" into our relationship with God. Surely the most holy place is the hardest, the most sacred mission is the one that takes us far from home, and the most meaningful calling is the one that tells me I'm made for more.

Benedictine monks take a vow of stability, committing to stay in one monastery for a lifetime. The contemplative Thomas Merton wrote:

> By making a vow of stability, the monk renounces the vain hope of wandering off to find a "perfect monastery." This implies a deep act of faith: the recognition that it does not much matter where we are or whom we live with, provided we can devote ourselves to prayer, enjoy a certain amount of silence, poverty, and solitude, work with our hands, read and study the things of God, and above all love one another as Christ has loved us. Stability becomes difficult for a man whose monastic ideal contains some note, some element of the extraordinary. All monasteries are more or less ordinary. The monastic life is by its very nature "ordinary." Its ordinariness is one of its greatest blessings.[1]

Saint Benedict knew the power of stability when it came to developing long-lasting community—roots will never grow when we keep transplanting ourselves. Jonathan Wilson-Hartgrove shares a story in his book *The Wisdom of Stability* about a man who confronted his pastor about his dissatisfaction with the church. Although the church had a reputation for taking community seriously, it wasn't meeting this man's expectations. The pastor listened, then asked him, "How long have you been here, again?"

"About a year," the man said.

"Then I guess you've got about a year's worth of community," his pastor said matter-of-factly. "Stay another year and you'll have two years' worth. Stay thirty and you might find some of what you're looking for."[2]

I confess I yearn for the thirty-year fruit without putting thirty years of time, tedium, and treasure into the ground. But God often urges us to do the hard work of staying before hospitality sparks true community.

* * *

One month after graduating from college, I accepted a job teaching junior high students at a low-income school in North Lawndale on Chicago's West Side. In 2001, North Lawndale was (and still is) one of the most poverty-stricken neighborhoods in Chicago. One hundred percent of the students at the school were black. When asked to sketch their neighborhood, my sixth graders drew, colored, and labeled street corners where drugs were sold, sex was bought, and guns were shot.

Since I'd graduated midyear, the school had been in session for months, and rumor had it that two teachers before me had already run off. I'm mortified to confess that I watched the movie *Dangerous Minds* the week after I took the job. In it, Michelle Pfeiffer challenges and engages her students in the magic of learning. I was determined to be inspirational. Secretly, I couldn't wait to be the hero.

In my passion to be a do-gooder, I added clutter to an already chaotic and confusing system. Bless my newly graduated heart, I sure tried. I quickly memorized students' names, worked sixteen-hour-days, planned elaborate lessons, and called my students' homes daily. When my students cursed at me, I told them I cared for them. But did I really? I promised I wouldn't abandon them—no matter how much they tried to get rid of me. I thought if they knew I was in it for the long haul they'd start to trust me.

But it wasn't enough. Despite toiling through the summer to plan curriculum for the fall, the week before school began, I received a message from the principal: "Come and get your things. We're sorry, but another teacher has been hired to replace you." Was it because I couldn't control my classroom? Had parents complained about me? Were there politics within the school that I wasn't privy to?

Or did my students and the administration sense my lack of authenticity? When I *thought* I was communicating love, did they feel patronized? Was I forcing the students into my culture, when I should have first bent and conformed to them? Perhaps my students and the administration saw through my idealism, my lust to be the hero who rushed in to save the day. I'll never know.

The middle school science teacher who had recruited me right out of college was also white, but her experience was vastly different from mine. Karen had a pixie cut, athletic build, and a quick smile, and as she showed me around on my first visit, she told me her dreams for the school and for the middle school students. At thirty-one, she and her husband had lived in a two-story walk-up in Lawndale for almost ten years and had informally adopted three boys. Her husband worked full-time in the neighborhood. Karen had a patience, optimism, and compassion I admired.

Their family still lives in Lawndale today—nearly thirty years later. Their adopted children are grown and their two biological children are two of just a few white children in their school. Her husband started businesses around the city that provide young men and women with jobs. As much as possible, Mike and Karen have assimilated into the neighborhood. They have allowed themselves not only to be known, but to know their neighbors.

In retrospect, I believe my mistake was telling myself I was all in without physically moving into the neighborhood. While my students sidestepped hazards on their short walks home every day, I commuted back to my safe apartment in my safe neighborhood fifty minutes north. I thought I could make a difference from a distance. And my students, the principal, and the other teachers saw what I could not yet see: I was in it for me.

Mike and Karen Trout were influenced by Wayne Gordon, or "Coach," who started Lawndale Community Church. Along with civil rights leader John Perkins, Gordon is one of the cofounders of the Christian Community Development Association (CCDA), an organization that hosts conferences and provides training for those doing urban ministry. Gordon encourages those who want to do urban ministry to commit at least fifteen years to the communities where they want to work, and says that longer is even better.[3] Most of us are not willing to commit one year to anything, much less fifteen. As a new graduate, I was eager to go, but I was less enthusiastic about promising to stay somewhere for even a year.

In most communities, the ones who make a difference are not the ones who swoop in to save the day but the ones who stay.

What happens when goers stay? When we counter culture and plant ourselves in neighborhoods, churches, marriages, and messy relationships? What happens when we let the Spirit infuse our staying with purpose, tuning our ears to the needs of others? How does this affect our relationships, our awareness of our surroundings, and our sense of belonging?

* * *

I nursed my infant with one arm that turned numb and madly scribbled notes with the other hand. When Isaiah was twelve days old and we were still renting a house in a small city south of Fort Collins, Colorado, I had secured him in the car seat and driven twenty miles to hear Bryan Stevenson speak at the university. His book, *Just Mercy*, about unjustly incarcerated adults and children, women and men, had exploded my inner life in the best and worst of ways. It was among the first books I read about racial and social injustices that hadn't just happened in the past but that were happening in the present. In the fog of those postpartum days, I recall little other than two words that threw my life back into alignment with the larger plan of God. Those words rang out as I read books, articles, and Bible verses in the coming weeks: "Get proximate," Stevenson told the audience.

Stevenson said we can't love people we can't see. Yes, we can read books, watch films, and diversify our social media feeds. But if we're sequestered in our houses in segregated neighborhoods, how are we to know—much less love—the people on the margins of society?[4] Soon after that, I read *The Power of Proximity* by Michelle Warren, who currently works for the CCDA. She and her husband intentionally moved into a low-income, mostly immigrant neighborhood in Denver when they were in their twenties. She challenges her readers to abandon comfort for the call to live in neighborhoods that privileged members of the dominant culture consider "unsafe."[5]

In her book, Warren talks about how Paul used his privilege in the Bible to spread the message of Jesus by using his network, connections, and knowledge of the culture to move in very different circles than an uneducated, non-Roman citizen would have access to. She writes, "Privileged people will listen to privileged people. You have a voice."[6] I wondered how I could steward my privilege to serve and honor others.

Although some people in the United States and other Western countries have never moved more than an hour away from their hometown by choice, others stay because they don't have the luxury of moving anywhere else. But no matter where we live—whether in the suburbs, a high-rise condo, or a remote farming community—our neighbors need hope, love, and practical hospitality.

Many of us do enjoy the gift of mobility. We can decide where we live, whom we live among, and how intentional we are about noticing and getting to know the strangers around us. John Perkins challenges followers of Jesus to use this gift of mobility to start a "quiet revolution" where Christians, like Mike and Karen Trout and Michelle Warren and her husband, are committed to inner growth as well as relevant outreach.

Perkins proposes doing this through the "three Rs of the quiet revolution: *relocation, reconciliation, and redistribution*." He says, "We must relocate the body of Christ among the poor and in the area of need." Next, "we must reconcile ourselves across racial and cultural barriers." And finally, "we must as Christians seek justice by coming up with means of redistributing goods and wealth to those in need."[7]

Although most humans prefer security and comfort, at times we must deliberately put ourselves on paths we'd rather avoid. Sometimes Jesus leads us to follow him to forsake freedom, fortune, and thrones to kneel in the dust. Whether by physically moving to a new location to live among those on the margins, volunteering in a homeless shelter or transition home, or opening our eyes to the poverty around us, proximity requires intentionality. The gift of mobility can lure us toward unhealthy forms of individualism, privacy, and independence—or can allow us to plant ourselves in communities of people who have just as much to teach as they do to receive.

The year after reading Michelle Warren's book, I met with her on the patio of a pizza restaurant in Denver, where she shared two "Michelle-isms" she teaches her children. The first is "Don't forget the poor." It's difficult to ignore the poor when you encounter them on a daily basis. The second is "You are the light of world, so don't be afraid. When you see darkness, run toward it with the light!"

Sipping ice water during my meal with Michelle, I thought of my calling when I was sixteen years old, and how life is nothing like what I envisioned. We now have a mortgage for our 1970s split-level home in Fort Collins, some savings, and a life insurance policy. We have grass to mow, and spruce, apple, and linden trees to keep alive. We own two cars, three strollers, and too many kitchen appliances. Our neighborhood is safe enough for kids to sprint back and forth between houses without an adult in sight, but not so safe I'd let them hang out alone at the neighborhood park my kids first dubbed "Trash Park," where I've found broken glass, syringes, and used condoms.

After I listened to Bryan Stevenson's lecture, we purposefully moved to our current neighborhood because it contains more socioeconomic diversity than other neighborhoods in our city. Our neighborhood has blocks and blocks of apartments and senior living condos, and our house is three miles from the university and near a bus line. I believe the Holy Spirit is just as active here as the Spirit is in the slums of Kampala, the orphanage in Tajikistan, and the house church in China. Like Dorothy in *The Wizard of Oz*, I've also learned our adventures sometimes lead us right back to where we started—to noticing the people in our home, down our street, and right in our own front yards.

While some of us may be led to move, go, and pledge ourselves to other lands, most of us are tasked with the mission to stay. What if we took that same sense of purpose and calling we often attribute to cross-cultural workers, pastors, and missionaries, and poured it into our right-here, right-now lives? What if we weren't made for *more* after all? What if we were made for *this*?

What happens when we choose to stay for fifteen, twenty, or thirty years—in a neighborhood, with a spouse, at a church? What if resistance to selling out actually looks like staying put? What happens to the depth of community when hospitality is not just a one-time event but a lifetime of recurring invitations?

As a teenager, I romanticized goers of the Bible like Abraham and Moses, Peter and Paul. In Bible studies we tend to focus on those who were sent, but what about those who stayed—opening their doors, hosting, and inviting strangers to sleep in their homes? When Jesus sent out twelve, and then seventy disciples, he commanded them to stay in people's homes and to shake the dust off their feet if they weren't welcomed. In Acts, seven men were appointed to stay back to ensure that those on the margins were seen. No less spiritual than the goers, one of the stayers named Stephen was described as a man full of "faith and of the Holy Spirit" and of "God's grace and power" (Acts 6:5, 8). Stephen delivered a powerful sermon right before he became the first known martyr for the Christian faith.

God poured power into the stayers just as much as into the goers. But more importantly, God loved them just the same. In the documentary *Won't You Be My Neighbor?*, Mr. Rogers says, "You don't ever have to do anything sensational for people to love you."[8] For a goer learning how to stay, that is good news. But the greater news comes from trusting that we don't ever have to do anything sensational for *God* to love us.

* * *

The month before we moved from our rental home of two years to the house we bought in Fort Collins, I spent most days slathering the walls, cabinets, and furniture of the empty house with paint. Two nights before the move, I sprawled out with the kids on the floor of the basement room we hoped to rent out to an international student. I read the kids a picture book about a dragon, then picked up where we left off in *The Jesus Storybook Bible*.

"This is one of my favorites," I told the kids, removing the red ribbon bookmark. I read aloud as they leaned against me. In the story from Luke 7, a woman tentatively tiptoes into the room, carrying her alabaster jar of perfume, likely her most valuable possession. She hears whispers and titters as she approaches Jesus. Exposing herself to ridicule and criticism, she continues with what she's compelled to do. In defiance of the lack of hospitality shown to Jesus by his hosts, she breaks her jar, pours perfume onto Jesus' feet, washes them with her tears, and wipes them with her hair. Jesus silences those who protest, commanding respect for what she is doing, for it is beautiful to him.

The kids seemed unmoved, but I paused to reflect, because that alabaster jar has represented something different in every season of my life so far. My Most Precious Thing, which Paul Tillich calls our "holy waste," had been my studies, my teaching career, my desire for marriage, my calling to China, my singleness, my independence, my children, and even my writing.[9] Each one, in its own time, smashed at the feet of Jesus. In the West, many of us possess the treasures of freedom, choice, mobility, privacy, independence, education, and self-betterment. Perhaps instead of holding them close, we're meant to look for ways to dash them at Jesus' feet.

In the days while we were in negotiations for our house, I had gone on a run that turned into a walk through a dry field. I prayed about our weighty decision to buy a house. As I strolled, I avoided potholes and divots in the path and suddenly prayed that our home would be a sanctuary. The word surprised me, because it is not how I would describe our life right now. With three tiny kids, chaotic, loud, and messy would be better descriptors. But the word *sanctuary* came to mind: A haven for the lost, lonely, afraid, or alone. A place to breathe in and out and to invite others to do the same. A landing pad for goers to stay. Solid ground to offer our family and guests a little bit of security in a shaky world.

No matter where we live, our homes can be a sanctuary for someone. There's a popular Danish word, *hygge* (pronounced "hooga"), that has appeared frequently in news articles and on social media. While most references to this word involve an individual cuddled up with fuzzy socks and a plush throw blanket next to a crackling fireplace, the word means "to cozy around *together*." Those living in Denmark—reported as a place where the people are happiest in the world—view *hygge* as a way of living in community with others. Less about solitude and self-care, the concept of *hygge* involves "being in each other's company in a cozy atmosphere."[10] Whether we are opening our homes or receiving hospitality from others, having a stable sanctuary can weld us together in relationship.

I didn't realize it at the time, but in the first year of living in our new home, we would host a family from Iran for nearly a week. Just a few weeks later, an Indian woman would move in with us for six months, inviting her parents to stay for two weeks at the end of her lease. After that, a grad student from Ghana would move in, whose initial four-month lease would become two years. The house would be a place for children to crash in and out of our backyard gate, for neighbors to gather for parties and cookouts, for weary moms to drop off their children to play, and where my husband and I would wake long before dawn to seek sanctuary before the chaos of the day began. Sharing our home would also mean less storage in the fridge and cabinets, a frequently crowded kitchen, self-consciousness over my kids clattering and banging on the floor above the guest room, and having to boot my parents to a hotel when they came to visit. With a commitment to hospitality comes the sacrifice of comfort and control.

Sitting on the basement floor with my children, I reflected on how I was once enamored by the allure of a life bursting with meaning and purpose. I had once followed Jim and Elisabeth Elliot all the way from balmy, alligator-infested Florida to a Christian liberal arts college in the Midwest. The Elliots were long gone by the time I got there, but Elisabeth's books about her martyred husband and her subsequent ministry as a missionary in Quito, Ecuador, inspired me to follow in their stead. As a high school student, I scribbled a quote by Jim Elliot on a note card that later hung in my dorm room and was copied into journal after journal over the next twenty years: "Wherever you are, be all there. Live to the hilt every situation you believe to be the will of God."

That quotation followed me into and out of Uganda, into and out of Chicago, into and out of China, back to Chicago into the arms of an actor, and finally across the United States to a simple home in Colorado. It turns out that the enigmatic will of God cloaks itself in a variety of languages, cultures, and stages of life. And sometimes, when we're out of breath and weary from the wandering, God calls us to stop going, searching, seeking, traveling, exploring, researching, and branching out and just start staying.

As the kids began fidgeting, I glanced at the trim I'd spent all month painting. I shook my head as I realized what I'd done. I'd covered the entire home with paint the color of "alabaster white." Every edge, corner, and ceiling a symbol of my treasures shattered at the feet of Jesus. This place, too, was holy ground.

The Guest is God.

—Hindu saying

THREE

Stranger Love

The aroma of cloves and sandalwood floated into the garage as I unloaded the kids from the minivan. Priya must be home, I thought. From photos, I knew her brother and parents used to sit cross-legged on the floor of their home in India performing Hindu rituals while smoke from incense curled into question marks toward the ceiling. Unused to the odor even after five months of Priya living with us, I sometimes plugged the air vent in our bedroom with a towel at night.

"Can we go down and see Priya?" Elijah asked, unvelcroing his shoes and tossing them into the bin by the door.

I agreed, shooing the kids downstairs as I wrestled the cutting board out of the cupboard and defrosted meat for supper. One-year-old Isaiah followed his older siblings, slinking backward down the stairs in one fluid motion.

On a repurposed nightstand in her bedroom, Priya displayed a small brass figurine, incense sticks, and offerings to other gods. She asked the kids not to touch the altar, so instead they swiveled round and round on her black leather office chair and chattered nonstop as she finished her engineering homework for grad school.

When Priya's parents came to visit, they brought a stack of books on Hindu mythology to our children as a gift from India, so we spent several nights during their two-week visit reading Hindu stories about men named Akbar and Birbal. The kids loved these stories. As a follower of Jesus, I never imagined I'd have a Hindu altar to idols in my basement or read Hindu stories to my children.

The kids raced upstairs, Priya following with a grin on her face. I turned down my podcast and put down my knife.

"Watch this! Okay, Adeline, show your mommy," she said.

My three-year-old plopped down, jutted her legs out on the wooden floor, squeezed her eyes shut, and curved her tiny arms up into the air. Holding thumb and forefinger in a small orb, she chanted, "Ommmmm."

I laughed and began entertaining somewhat irrational superstitions. Would having an altar to idols somehow invite other spirits into our home? Did I want my children knowing that other religions worship multiple gods? Would the Holy Spirit be grieved by us welcoming someone of another religion into our home? Fear filled in the blanks of my ignorance with solid suspicion.

Or, another part of me wondered, was this a part of God's plan to use us in another's life and she in ours?

* * *

In the West, we can be fantastic goers—eager teens and earnest adults in matching T-shirts crowding planes, trains, and boats for summer mission trips to places we can't pronounce. For a few days or weeks, we serve the "sexy other"—those living in mud huts, ramshackle slums, and makeshift refugee camps. But do we love strangers at home? Living in another country, and having someone from another country actually live with me, unearthed layers of unease within myself. I can leap into adventure as long as it's on my own terms, but as soon as I must put aside my own comfort or control, I get grumpy. Having any stranger move in with us is a test of our true character. And I often fail the test.

As humans, we fear the strange, distrust the unknown, and shield ourselves from the unfamiliar. And yet the Greek word for hospitality used in the Bible, *philoxenos*, literally means "love (*philos*) of strangers (*xenos*)." Our generous God calls us to a bizarre hospitality that doesn't just invite friends and family to our tables but compels us to love even strangers. Love usurps fear in kingdom living. Or it should.

A cheeky man of the law attempted to stump Jesus after Jesus had narrowed the heartbeat of God down to two pulses: love God and love neighbor. In response to the man's question, "But who is my neighbor?" Jesus told the story of a man attacked on the way to Jericho. The beaten man lay there, unable to help himself. A priest came along but crossed to the other side of the road rather than help the injured man. Soon afterward, a Levite—an assistant priest, from a heritage known for its honor and holiness—also avoided the man and switched sides of the road rather than help another human being in distress. Finally, another traveler, from the despised lower class—a Samaritan—noticed the wounded man, gathered him onto his donkey, and took him to an inn.

"Who was a neighbor to the man?" Jesus asked.

"The man who stopped and helped him," the listener responded.

Here, in Luke 10:25-37, Jesus expanded the definition of neighbor from those who look, act, and think the way we do to those we may fear and who may fear us. Our neighbor is the person we meet on the way, calling out—usually at inconvenient times—for our attention, compassion, or help.

I confess I used to be—and still often am—a road-crosser, avoiding the people Jesus defines as my neighbor. In the United States, fanatical Islam dominates the news, while the quiet devotion of the young Saudi Muslim woman, Norah, who lived with us for a year in Chicago does not. I've experienced more selfless hospitality from Muslim friends in my life than I have from most followers of Christ. Countless times in the United States and in China, they, like the Samaritan, came to my aid, though they had many reasons to hate what I represent—a Western culture and Christian faith that seems to despise them. My Muslim students in China welcomed me to their villages, fed me, clothed me, and offered me their best even though their families had very little.

"I'm sure you'd do the same for me if I came to your country," the father of one of my Chinese Muslim students said confidently after I had thanked him for his hospitality. Smiling sadly, I knew the truth. Seventy-five percent of international students will never even enter an American home in all the years they study in the United States.[1]

Norah was the first international student to live with us. Back in Chicago, I had volunteered for a month at her oral English class at Loyola University. I brought my first baby, Elijah, who was just eight months old at the time. He would crawl around on the floor and help ease nerves as I chatted with shy Muslim women from Saudi Arabia. Some wore a full burka, the cloth over their mouths blowing out with their words; others no head covering at all; and others, like Norah, wore a solid-colored scarf wrapped turban-style.

After just a few weeks, Norah asked if she could live with us. She covered her mouth, hiding her braces as we talked about our arrangement. She wore tight jeans, a long navy-blue cardigan that hung midthigh, and canvas tennis shoes. She was barely five feet tall, and I'd learn that without her hijab, her hair fell almost to her waist. Her roommate situation wasn't ideal, and she thought she could learn English more quickly if she lived with an American family. Although the original arrangement was for four months, that morphed into ten months and culminated with her entire family of six sleeping on our living room floor one summer. I didn't know it at the time, but several years later she would study for a year in Colorado and accompany us on visits to Rocky Mountain National Park. I'd discover she had a sixth sense when it came to intuiting a person's character and intent. Our kids would grow up knowing her better than their real aunts, who lived in other states. They took to calling her Auntie Boo for all the times she played peekaboo with them as babies.

The month after Norah moved in with us, I hosted a Halloween party for six of her Saudi classmates. Having banished Adam from the apartment, I welcomed the young women and promised not to post photos on social media. They removed their hijabs and abayas, which had cloaked their shiny black hair, three-inch heels, and trendy designer clothes. They paired off to carve intricate designs into fat pumpkins.

"Have you been in an American home before?" I asked them.

None had. This was the first time for all of them, though many had lived in the United States for more than a year.

It's usually more comfortable to love people who look, think, and act the way we do. We get each other's jokes, sing each other's songs, and walk each other's paths. We share the same tome of pop culture, history, and experience. But if God had wanted us to be with people just like us, God wouldn't have taken the devout Jews—the people who prided themselves on being separate—and told them to be grafted together with the heathen Gentiles (Romans 11:17). God wouldn't have sculpted a church from every tribe, tongue, people, and nation and called it a unified body (Ephesians 3:6). Jesus wouldn't have commanded us to corporately devour his body, sip his blood, or breathe his Spirit and use it as a sign of our oneness in Christ (1 Corinthians 10:16-17).

As an expatriate living in China, I learned that being a stranger spotlights our insecurities and foibles, weaknesses and groanings, quirks and questions. I often didn't fit in or belong, and I possibly never would. Because of this, I knew what it was to be lonely, isolated, and misunderstood.

Many people in the West may not know what it feels like to stand out in a crowd. Some people may even need to put themselves in the position of being a stranger, newbie, or sojourner. Usually this happens organically as we are new students, parents, employees, church visitors, or travelers. Our empathy for strangers surges when we, too, know what it's like to flounder in unfamiliar and sometimes hostile waters.

I now watch a Chinese woman wandering the grocery store in the United States, caressing every oversized squash and cucumber, and I imagine she is comparing them to her vegetables back home. Perhaps she is thinking of long talks with familiar people while dicing cucumbers in a familiar kitchen. Perhaps she is thinking of buying vegetables in outdoor markets every day on her way home from work, and tossing the bags into the basket on her bicycle. In displaced strangers, we sometimes spy ourselves.

* * *

A homeless outreach in my city pairs a large church with a smaller church to host families who are homeless for a two-week period four times a year. When Isaiah was six months old, I left the kids with Adam and headed to the church we were attending at the time. Our job was to cook for the families and eat with them afterward. Stirring the German potato salad in the church kitchen right before dinner was ready, I thought, What if I say the wrong thing? Will we find anything in common?

Scanning the church multipurpose room, with a table set for six, I sat down next to a young Latina woman and her two children.

"How old are your kids?" I asked as we picked up our forks to begin eating.

"One and two," she said. "Twelve months apart."

I paused mid-bite. I thought of my six-month-old at home and self-consciously touched my still-soft belly. I couldn't fathom being pregnant again so soon after giving birth and blurted out without thinking, "Did you cry when you found out?"

She laughed. "Ooh, yes!"

In an instant, we connected over the shock of having a months-old baby and discovering you're pregnant again. Friendships often fuse at the intersection of our deepest fears, our greatest longings, and sometimes even our human hilarities.

She was a single mom, while I had a husband at home. She transported her kids by bicycle and bike trailer, while I drove my kids around in a five-year-old minivan. She was homeless, while we had just toured a four-bedroom home.

Yet I understood her fierce love for her children. I inherently identified with the determination she had to protect them. I respected her for doing what it took to feed and clothe them. In that moment, we walked a bridge not because I know what it's like to be homeless, but because we knew what it's like to be mothers. Because we knew what it's like to be human beings. And because she met me in the middle with her story.

Fear fades when strangers have quirks, tattoos, and hobbies. When we know names of mothers, fathers, sisters, brothers, sons, and daughters. Noticing a slouching teenager on the street, I am not afraid, because in him, I see the face of Tony, the boy who was my student in Chicago, or Dominic, the kid from the youth group where I volunteered. When I pass a mother with a baby begging on the side of the road, or see the picture of a mother on the news after being separated from her child, I swim the universal ache of every mother who has entered a real or imagined nightmare, terrified for her child.

* * *

As a mom to three tinies, I sometimes feel that life is a tight bubble with little space for strangers, ministries, or service outside my family. Even though we've attempted to get proximate to those at the fringes of society, privacy still separates us from those who are suffering. When I lived in urban areas in China and Chicago, poverty paraded in plain sight, but even there, living near those who were different from me didn't guarantee relationship. For me as an educated, white, middle-class woman, noticing poverty and knowing its name were not synonymous. Living in passive proximity to need doesn't necessarily mean love crosses barriers by osmosis.

Because I'm a nerd, I recently sketched a circular diagram of the people I think God is calling me to love. My husband takes the center, then my children, extended family, church members, coworkers, and neighbors (although if I'm being honest, this idea is based more on natural instinct than on any actual words of Jesus). Those I won't know unless I intentionally seek them out hover on the fringes of my life circle. Often, these people are "the other" in society—the outcast, misfit, incarcerated, orphaned, widowed, elderly, institutionalized, displaced, hospitalized, marginalized, or feared. As I did this exercise, I realized I fixate 99 percent of my time and attention on loving family and friends, while Jesus specifically implores his followers to love misfits, outcasts, and sinners (see Luke 5:32). At the end of the day and especially at the end of the week, I have little emotional energy left to extend to those on the margins. So how do I reconcile that reality with the heart of Jesus, which is decidedly *for* people on the edges of society?

I had been feeling guilty about this, and I wondered if I should volunteer at a homeless shelter, pregnancy center, or elderly home or with a program to help prisoners reenter society. On a run one morning, I thought about Jesus' story of the Samaritan. Wide, empty roads sloped downward to more wide roads as my feet pounded the street and the cold air cut my face. I wondered why the Samaritan was traveling to Jericho to begin with. I assumed he must have had business there, because he paid an innkeeper to watch over the injured man so he could get back to what he was doing.[2] He was busy just living his life when he came across an interruption in his path.

And then it hit me. The Samaritan didn't need to change roads to encounter God. He was walking his road, minding his business, when God brought someone into his path. And then he had a choice: notice and do something, or ignore and move along.

Stay on your Jericho road, Leslie, God seemed to say. *Pay attention to the people on the side of your road. Stop trying to veer over onto everyone else's roads.*

While we sometimes need to change roads and seek out places to volunteer and serve, other times God wants us to notice the people on the roads where we already travel. Slowing to a walk, I felt the weighted blanket of guilt lift off my shoulders. It wasn't that I was supposed to *do* more, but that God wanted me to notice the people the Spirit was placing on my path.

Suddenly I remembered a woman I had talked to the day before. I had chatted with Susan as our boys dueled with sticks and climbed the tree outside the preschool building. She told me she is a single parent for her five children. She struggled to manage all their schedules and often wondered what to do with her youngest child.

While I had been googling for volunteer and ministry opportunities, God had already put someone on my Jericho road. The next time I saw her, we sat on my ratty old picnic blanket and watched the kids play tag on the lawn after school. She mentioned their hectic day and I took a chance.

"Hey, I was thinking," I said. "Your son is welcome to come to our house whenever you need. My kids would love it."

"Really?" she said. "That would be amazing."

I had been so busy hijacking other people's Jericho roads that I hadn't even noticed God directing a spotlight on someone beside the road I walk every single day.

* * *

My fifth year in China, I sat cross-legged on the couch and focused on Hannah, my Chinese friend, as she spoke in Mandarin Chinese. She and her husband, Sam, loved Jesus and oriented their entire lives around him. They had quit their jobs the year before to focus on ministry to college students and start a house church. They had even moved in with a couple having marital problems to help them navigate their conflict together in one house. Sam described his faith as being "dominated by Jesus."

"There seem to be so many people who need love and attention," I whined to Hannah. "How do you know who to focus on—friends, family, church people, the needy?" I asked. "I get overwhelmed trying to figure out how to spend my time."

"You pray for the *pang bien de ren*," she said, which means "the right-next-to-you people." She glanced out the window before she continued, "And then you wait and see who God brings into your life."

You pray for the right-next-to-you people. I exhaled. She had made it sound so simple. And yet I knew that prayer tenderizes our hearts toward people we might not naturally love or notice.

In our new neighborhood in Colorado, I'm keeping track of who lives where. *The Art of Neighboring* calls this "neighborhood mapping."[3] That seemed a bit too structured and formal for me, so instead I jot down the names of neighbors in a notebook when I learn them. Then I pray for them when I pass their home.

In his letter to the Colossian church, Paul tells them to "devote yourselves to prayer, being watchful and thankful"

(Colossians 4:2). We pray, then watch and give thanks for what we see. Just a few verses later, Paul adds a fourth idea: "Be wise in the way you act toward outsiders; make the most of every opportunity" (v. 5). The practice of prayer transforms apathy to awareness and callousness to sensitivity toward both outsiders and opportunities.

* * *

Patting my frizzy, dyed-brown hair and flimsy black glasses with one hand, I adjusted the towel under my shirt with the other. I was ready. All the youth group leaders were in costume, scattered around Navy Pier in Chicago for a human scavenger hunt. The teenagers would soon be on the move. I grabbed the broom and dustpan I had borrowed from the janitor at school and glided it around the edges of trashcans, gates, and guard rails. Glancing around nervously, I congratulated myself on my wise choice of "uniform," since the other grounds workers also wore khaki pants and polo shirts. I hope none of them discover me, I thought, moving in the opposite direction of the other workers.

"Where's the bathroom?" a man asked abruptly. I spun around, slightly stunned.

"Uh, I think it's over there," I said, pointing. "I'm new here," I lied, almost too quickly. I hadn't anticipated having to answer questions.

The first cluster of youth group teenagers were approaching. I hung my head and swept up cigarette butts and discarded Dorito bags, then lifted the scooper to dump them in the large black bin. The kids passed within four feet of me and kept walking.

I swept around kiosks that sold overpriced key chains, gaudy beer openers, and jeweled cell phone cases. I glanced up just as another group from our youth group passed. They kept walking.

When the time came for the scavenger hunt to end, I found the McDonald's we were supposed to meet at and spotted the youth kids crowded around a table, scarfing down fries and laughing loudly. I pushed the broom between their sandaled feet, poking at the trash below.

"Excuse me, can I sweep under your feet? Thanks," I murmured. They swung their legs to the side to avoid my broom.

So this is what it feels like to be invisible, I thought. No one sees me, notices, or cares. No one looks at an overweight, unattractive janitor sweeping up chewing gum and cheese popcorn in a crowded tourist area. I swept around the entire table without a single teenager noticing I was the youth group leader who had worked with them for three years.

* * *

Jesus sidled up to those who were invisible to the rest of society. Easing through a crowd, he sensed power escape him when a chronically ill woman brushed the edge of his cloak with her fingers. "Who touched me?" he demanded. He was attuned to the individual voice of a leper crying out among a cacophony of other voices, "Jesus, Son of David, have mercy on me!" He conversed with a woman at a well even though she was an outcast in society. (See Luke 8:43-48; 18:35-43; John 4:1-42.)

Jesus hoofed it over to a sycamore tree after noticing a man who had clambered up to get a better view. Instead of passing by or ignoring the hated man—a criminal—Jesus stopped what he was doing, stepped off the path, and spoke to him. "Zacchaeus, come down!" He took the encounter even further, inviting himself over to his house. "I'm coming to your house today!" Jesus said. I imagine he said it with a grin and a wink, tickled to confound the onlookers. I'm sure Zacchaeus was delighted that Jesus not only noticed him but wanted to share a meal with him and his family (see Luke 19:1-10).

* * *

One spring evening in China, I waited for the bus at rush hour. There were no lines, no "I was here firsts," and no personal space, just a giant mob of humanity moving and rippling as one. Not in a hurry, I sat on the bench, my arms fatigued from carrying packages I had picked up from the post office. I watched with amusement as strangers threw elbows and knees to force their way onto the bus, a wave of people lapping into a narrow tide pool. As the bus approached, the crowd moved in unison, attempting to leap into the small opening, with most being left behind, ebbing back onto the sidewalk as the bus moved down the street.

One man in particular caught my eye. He looked like a caricature of the Chinese men I knew, with a floppy coat and pants. His shaggy hair shaded his eyes and his shoulders slumped like an insecure teenager. As the bus approached, he rushed the crowd, pressing his body behind eager would-be riders, then retreated seconds before the bus idled away. I eyed him intently, wondering why he never pushed his way onto the bus. Then I saw why.

As he pressed in, his hands moved quickly, jutting in between bodies, quietly ransacking pockets, pants, and purses. Eventually, the man noticed me on the bench, lap piled high with packages, playing investigative reporter to his every move. I finally scraped up the nerve to speak to him.

"So how much money do you make in a day?" I asked when he stood just feet away from me.

Without hesitation or even looking at me, he responded, "Over one thousand yuan a day." I tried not to gasp. This was easily a month's wages for a lower- to middle-class Chinese person in my city at that time.

Another bus approached. He glanced past me. "Excuse me," he said in Chinese. "I need to get back to work." I watched him run up against the crowd again, then retreat at the last moment. We chatted between each of his little "work trips," and I asked about his home, his family, and if he felt bad about what he was doing.

"Mei ban fa," he said. "No other way."

When the crowds subsided, I kept a hand on my bag and bid my new acquaintance goodbye.

"Man zou," he said. "Go slowly."

"Man zou," I replied.

When Jesus saw a person, he saw a soul made in God's image, with God's qualities and characteristics. "You look like me!" is how *The Jesus Storybook Bible* has Jesus saying it. "You're the most beautiful thing I've ever made!"[4] Jesus noticed people the rest of society wanted to forget.

I didn't tell the Chinese thief about God, reprimand him for being a criminal, or even see him again—although I did warn a few people to guard their wallets as they got on the bus, pointing out the man in the long coat with darting arms. Unlike Jesus, I didn't invite myself over to his home. But sitting there and observing an illegal activity right in front of my eyes that I wouldn't have noticed otherwise was illuminating. And I wondered how much humanity I usually miss.

* * *

Dorothy Day was a journalist, activist, and Catholic convert. She wrote that "giving shelter or food to anyone who asks for it, or needs it, is giving to Christ."[5] She believed the strangers that she and her Catholic Worker sisters and brothers welcomed into their homes of hospitality were not only representatives of Jesus. She believed they *were* Jesus.

Day wrote, "God made heaven hinge on the way we act toward Him in His disguise of commonplace, frail, ordinary humanity—it is not a duty to help Christ, it is a privilege."[6] Because of this, she and her companions were not discriminating in whom they served.

In Jesus' revolutionary Sermon on the Mount, he spun the Jewish law in a dizzying deconstruction of all his listeners once knew. Give to the person who asks to borrow from me? Okay, maybe. But love my enemy? Jesus took it even further as he preached, "If you love those who love you, what reward will you get? Are not even the tax collectors doing that? And if you greet only your own people, what are you doing more than others? Do not even pagans do that?" (Matthew 5:46-47). Jesus pointed out their love-for-love equations and called them bogus and unremarkable. Audacious love seeks to love even the unlovable, the ugly, and the hated.

Dorothy Day and a couple of her companions spent time in jail for protesting. She appreciated the experience because it helped her to love with greater empathy. But she still struggled to love people who were challenging to love. As a practice, she would tell herself, "Jesus is _____ (insert name of hard person to love)."[7] Do we see the face of Jesus in those who are hardest for us to love?

Jesus is <u>name of the politician I despise</u>.
Jesus is <u>the immigrant from a certain country</u>.
Jesus is <u>name of family member who doesn't understand me</u>.
Jesus is <u>the criminal</u>.
Jesus is <u>my coworker who tells offensive jokes</u>.

Loving those at the center of our life circle diagrams is nothing revolutionary. Loving those we despise, or those who may despise us, is what takes Christianity from ordinary to outrageous.

* * *

One of the most haunting passages of Scripture is in Matthew 25, when Jesus describes returning in glory with all his angels. In the scene, King Jesus ascends the throne and all the nations gather before him. He separates them, sectioning the "sheep" off to his right and the "goats" to his left. Jesus invites those on his right—the sheep—to come and inherit the kingdom prepared for them from the foundation of the world. He discloses why they deserve such a gift—and it is not for the reasons they thought.

He says,

> I was hungry and you gave me something to eat,
> I was thirsty and you gave me something to drink,
> I was a stranger and you invited me in,
> I needed clothes and you clothed me,
> I was sick and you looked after me,
> I was in prison and you came to visit me.
> (Matthew 25:35-36)

The listeners are confused. "When, Lord?" they ask. They don't remember feeding, housing, clothing, healing, or visiting a king.

"Truly I tell you, whatever you did for one of the least of these brothers and sisters of mine, you did for me," the king answers (v. 40).

What if we went searching for Jesus not only in the parks, grocery stores, coffee shops, and public libraries, but also in the alleys, homeless shelters, hospitals, and jails? People in Jesus' time often didn't recognize him, although he was in plain sight. His own disciples thought he was a ghost when they didn't recognize him after the resurrection (see Luke 24:37). Mary Magdalene didn't know it was him until he spoke her name, and the men on the road to Emmaus didn't know who he was until he broke the bread as he hosted them in their own home (see John 20:14-16; Luke 24:13-35). Is it possible for Jesus to be in our midst and for us to miss him completely?

* * *

Priya, our Hindu guest, crammed colorful saris from floor to ceiling in her closet and spent weeks picking out her graduation dress. She giggled with girlish excitement when she told us her parents had booked a flight to the United States to see her walk across the stage and claim her graduate degree. She got in arguments with her boyfriend and binge-watched Netflix. She was so, so human. For six months we observed her, spoke with her, met her family, and ate her food. And as I shared a home with her, I began to understand that familiarity is the floodlight to fear's dark shadows.

Strangers are never strange to God. And they are only strange because we don't know them yet.

Hospitality grips us by the chin and turns our face to notice, serve, and honor humanity inside, outside, and on the wayside. Sometimes we invite people into our homes and lives, and sometimes we go out and join people in unfamiliar or uncomfortable spaces. But we always pray for peeled-back eyes to walk our Jericho roads, seeing and celebrating the souls along the way as Jesus in disguise.

A hasty person misses sweet things.

—Swahili proverb

FOUR

Linger Longer

On a date night during our third year in Colorado, Adam and I unwittingly strolled into an alternate reality. The shop in downtown Fort Collins called Swampgas and Gossamer piqued our interest, and we wandered into the museum of mystery. Corrugated metal, ancient pianos, giant springs, and twinkle lights were twisted into statues and seemingly abstract art installations. I poked around for price tags and discovered only more curiosities. Nothing was for sale.

"Strange Things for Strange People. Strangers Welcome," the sign in the window announced. As we crept into the store, I noticed a man hovering in the corner like the Cheshire Cat.

"Are you the creator and curator of all this?" Adam asked.

"I am," he answered, taking a step out of the shadows toward us and revealing he was in his seventies, with shoulder-length silver hair. "I'm Les Sunde," he said, extending his hand. "And who are you two?"

We drifted into easy conversation with Mr. Sunde, mesmerized by his odd perceptiveness. He told us about his inventions and suggested that his home outside the city was even more bizarre, with an entire carousel on the roof. I would later discover he lives in a school bus in his backyard and uses his home as an art studio.

He asked us questions and we shared a bit of our story, admitting we were still struggling to adapt to life in Colorado.

"Maybe you were supposed to move away from Chicago so it would reveal what's most important to you," he suggested, nodding to two guests who had just come into the shop. "Perhaps you were only meant to be here in Colorado for a time."

In our failure to choose a church or feel that we were a part of community, Adam and I had talked many times about this possibility. When is discontentment a sign that we should leave a place, a job, a school, or a dream? Maybe our inability to find our footing meant we should look for other options of places to live.

"Or"—he paused for a beat—"perhaps you just need to dive in and give this place a chance." We were listening. Although Mr. Sunde didn't seem to believe in a traditional God, perhaps God was opening his mouth and using Mr. Sunae to speak truth to us.

He continued. "Maybe Fort Collins will be like a poem you've read a million times. One day, a familiar line will leap from the page, finally capturing your senses." I grimaced. I didn't want that to be the answer. I still lacked the tenacity for Staying Put. Like a gardener abandoning her plants after one month of monotonous watering and weeding, I get bored before the first fruit emerges. But perhaps I could learn to channel my wandering within the boundaries of my own landscape.

* * *

Loitering and lingering are sometimes the best practices for falling in love with home and other humans. Late author and writing instructor Brenda Ueland dubbed this "moodling."[1] Sometimes we bump into angels of absurdity—like Mr. Sunde—as we moodle, dawdle, and dally close to home. Wandering whets our appetite for wonder. But while wandering blind delivers bruised shins, wandering wide-eyed can increase our gratitude for the people we live among and the unique spaces we share.

When we moved Elijah from a crib to a twin bed, he suddenly refused to nap. As a mom dependent on that hour or two to regroup and regain my sanity, I was desperate for a respite in my day. At the time we'd only been in Colorado a couple of months and I hadn't done much exploring. So every day for weeks, I snapped the kids in their car seats (thank God for a legal way to strap down my children in one place) and drove. The tires lulled the children to sleep as my phone's GPS guided us along the foothills through fields dotted with horses, llamas, and fluffy alpacas at pasture. I thought and prayed, but mostly soaked in silence. It felt like rehydrating after weeks of aridity.

High in the hills where red rock formations sloped sideways, I'd often lose the signal on my phone and have to reorient myself home. On some drives I wove the car in and out up to Estes Park through the canyon of the Big Thompson River, where bighorn sheep scaled the craggy cliffs carved by the river. If the kids woke up, I'd tell them, "Look for the sheep! They're probably camouflaged. I have to watch the road, but you can search for them—look carefully, I bet you'll be able to find one." Once, I caught a glimpse of a sign spray-painted on the rocks near the bottom of the canyon: "Linger Longer," it suggested.

Linger longer.

What do we find when we linger longer? Before we can offer hospitality to others, we have to spot the camouflaged people—much like those bighorn sheep I encouraged my children to search for—hiding in plain sight. In all the places I've lived, I've noticed a strange, symbiotic relationship: when we begin to love people, we begin to love a place.

* * *

Lingering in Mr. Sunde's shop reminded me that curiosity often helps us to see comedy in the commonplace. Stoking a sense of humor was one of my main coping mechanisms in China and Uganda on days when being an outsider felt unbearable. Chickens flapping around on the bus floor and T-shirts with humorous English translations could usually make me laugh. International visitors to the United States sometimes find what I consider ordinary and normal to be puzzling and funny. A Chinese couple I met on a train ride to Shanghai once told me about their first visit to the United States. They had stood watching traffic at a four-way stop for an hour, astounded and baffled. How did all those drivers know what to do? And on two separate occasions, our international friends have laughed at the flocks of wild geese wandering the Walmart parking lots. "There's no way those geese would still be alive in our country!" one said. We can discover delight in any culture, but also in our own—if we're paying attention.

As I peered around at the old parts Mr. Sunde had fused together to create new inventions, I thought of the City Museum in Saint Louis. On one of our road trips to Chicago, we had made a detour to the fantastical, four-floor playground designed by artists for kids and adults alike. Mr. Sunde would have approved of the museum's goal to promote childlike wonder in every guest. A sign at the ticket counter boasted "No Maps," leaving guests to wander their way through tunnels, down the ten-story slide, and to the mini circus on the second floor.

As we settled into our seats in the museum's small auditorium, a clown ran out and sprawled face-first onto the carpet. Elijah laughed until he hiccupped as the clown kept making fun of herself and performing silly tricks. I glanced at Adam to assess his reaction. Did he think she was any good? Adam's current profession is voice acting and audio book narration, and he has a background in theater. He is a trained clown, with the weirdest résumé I've ever seen: "Certified to fight with rapier and dagger, rides unicycle, juggles three to four balls, torches, and knives." (One of my eighth-grade students in Chicago once printed it out and passed it around class while I tried to teach a literature class. After noticing the snickering, I intercepted the paper and had to admit that my husband is atypical on many levels.) Although I've never seen Adam perform as a clown, he has educated me—a nonactor—on the graces, glories, and deep meaning of clowning in the acting world.

Clowns dig up the ridiculous, creating comedy from wrinkles, blemishes, and awkward behaviors. Clowning reminds me of the verse in 1 Corinthians 1:27, about God using foolish and weak things to shame the wise. The theory behind clowning also echoes Matthew 18:3, where Jesus tells his followers to change and become like children. Like clowns, we who want to live meaningful lives can capitalize on every opportunity to be amused and can invite others to delight alongside us. Perhaps God wants us to stop taking ourselves so seriously. Perhaps playing, comedy, and laughter are our first steps in metamorphosing into the kingdom kids of Jesus' imagination.

* * *

"How do you start making a new piece of . . . art?" I asked Mr. Sunde, peering at the hundreds of metal inventions filling the shop with squeaks and spurts. It was a metal museum an author like Dr. Seuss might write about, with junk upcycled to evoke wonder.

"The main word I think about is being available," he said, looking around at his creations. "As a creator, you have to be available and on the prowl for potential. I can walk into a junk shop and find a treasure there. It speaks to me if I'm listening, telling me what it wants to be."

Available. For Mr. Sunde, being "available" translated to art. For the follower of Jesus, it could mean art, but also availability to the susurrations of the Spirit in our humdrum lives. On lonely days when we may feel out of place, it helps to see our cities as places God picked for us, our neighbors as eternal, and our kitchen sinks as habitations for the Spirit of God. Which people does God want us to notice? What wonders is God inviting us to explore? Are we available?

The poet Luci Shaw says we all—whether conscious of it or not—are swimming in waters of unknown depth.[2] I want to be conscious of the depths of the waters I swim. I want to linger long enough to grasp how God is using the natural world to invite me into the supernatural world even as I touch the fur-like ice on the wooden railing in the yard, return emails, or make yet another peanut butter sandwich.

Before China, marriage, and children, I used to reserve a day once or twice a year to battle either the bitter wind or the giddy tourists and roam the streets of downtown Chicago. I usually ended up meandering the hushed halls of the Chicago Institute of Art. Once there, I would seek out a particular painting. When I found it, I stood enchanted. In the painting, a woman in a headscarf stands barefoot in a dim field, her mouth slightly agape, her gaze transfixed, while the neon orange sun sets (or rises) in the distance. She holds a sickle in her right hand, and her left foot is slightly forward. She seems to be listening, arrested by a noise or thought, captured in a spell. The title of the piece, *The Song of the Lark*, solves the puzzle—the melody of a single songbird has bewitched her.

Shakespeare mentions the lark in "Sonnet 29." I wonder if the painter, Jules Breton, painted with these lines in mind:

> The lark at break of day arising
> from sullen earth, sings hymns at heaven's gate.[3]

Would the song of a single lark stop me in my tracks? Would I even notice, much less spin the song as a hymn for my Creator? Even Job in his agonies testifies to the voice of God reverberating through our natural world to capture our attention: "But ask the animals, and they will teach you, or the birds in the sky, and they will tell you; or speak to the earth, and it will teach you, or let the fish of the sea inform you. Which of all these does not know that the hand of the Lord has done this?" (Job 12:7-9). And what do the songbirds say? Perhaps they sing to remind us of the presence of God in the natural world right here and now, inviting us into a bigger story. Perhaps God rejoices over us as we grasp the gift of rootedness, pausing our menial work to delight in a lark ringing in the day.

* * *

Dust tinted my toes tangerine as I traipsed up the Ugandan village road to hail three different taxis. Chicken squawks, thudding drumbeats, and children's giggles echoed in the distance. For six months during my senior year of college, I volunteered with a child sponsorship project that supported over one hundred children from the slums of Kampala. The project provided school fees and vocational training, Bible study, and a hot meal of maize called *posho*, groundnut stew, and baby bananas every Saturday.

Weeks into living with a Ugandan family in a village forty-five minutes outside Kampala, going to work every day at the project office, and feeling buzzed by culture shock, I found I had little to offer in the way of practical skills. I didn't know the language, culture, or needs of the people. I was, in fact, likely to do more harm than good. And everybody knew it.

Awareness of my inadequacies reached a new low the day my Ugandan host mother questioned my ability to scrub the pots and pans alongside the housekeepers. The house had no indoor plumbing, so the two women hauled five-gallon containers of water up from the well at the bottom of the hill every day. I offered to help with washing dishes mostly so I didn't feel I was taking more than I was giving.

"But can you wash dishes?" My host mother looked at me dubiously. "Don't you have machines to do that in your country?"

Anger roiled in my veins at her suggestion that I was a precious, spoiled American. I resolved to prove her stereotypes about Americans all wrong. I woke at five the next morning and stubbornly stood at the outdoor table in the yard, my arms buried in soapy water up to my elbows, washing the dinner dishes and leaving them to drip-dry in the sun.

My host mother was also my supervisor at the child sponsorship project, and I complained that I felt useless there too. "But what can you do?" she asked, assigning me the mundane task of filing papers out in the leaning, rusted trailer used for extra office space.

Humility doesn't come naturally to overachievers like me. Pride pulls us up by our bootstraps, motivating us to take the next heroic step into the unknown. Until we can't. And we sit down in a slump, beaten by our own inadequacies and pride, and reevaluate our purpose. We finally find our true selves down there in the dust. Stop *doing*, God seems to whisper. Just *be*.

Lessening, it turns out, is a gift. It's a forced release of the burden to *do* more, to *be* more. It's a reminder of the merit of being last in line and first to bow as we learn to grovel at Jesus' table. God never loved me for the sensational thing I could do. God used my time in Uganda to teach me the value of just *being*.

It took me days of furious filing before I stopped fuming and started noticing the people around me. I wasn't the only one in that tipsy old trailer. Two other Ugandan women worked at their desks, and there was, it turned out, plenty of time to talk. My host mother dialed up my pride to an uncomfortable level, sending me scurrying for my identity in the African dirt. But when I finally looked up beyond myself, I noticed that the beauty wasn't in the doing but in the knowing. It was in the noticing of people. It was, as author Mike Mason says, in the practicing of their presence.[4] The tasks weren't the focal point. The point was always the people.

* * *

"Does each piece have a story behind it?" I asked Mr. Sunde, sensing the night stretching past my usual bedtime. He nodded, and without cracking a smile, told us the story of his machine that travels backward but not forward in time, a bicycle fueled by laughter, and a machine that put the purr in cats. Trying not to laugh myself, I felt like a guest in Willy Wonka's chocolate factory. "The junk isn't what's important, actually," he explained earnestly, "but what moves it. The story behind the junk."

I glanced around. Sure enough, either by battery, electricity, or hand crank, every installation moved. The story moves the junk. The mention of story reminded me of a time when I had gone window-shopping with Adam in Wicker Park in Chicago. We were newly engaged, and it had been just a few months since I moved back to Chicago from China. As we strolled down the sidewalk, we bumped into one of Adam's old actor friends asking passersby to sign a petition for animal rights. Adam introduced me to the lanky guy wearing a backward baseball cap over stringy hair.

"So what's your story?" he asked me almost immediately. He tucked his clipboard under his arm and leaned his back against the storefront window without any intention of moving until I had spilled my entire life story.

His question put a stopper in the door of the conversation, allowing me to share what I wanted to awkwardly blurt out to every stranger I met at that time of my life—that I had recently returned from China and was devastated by the loss. So much better than "What do you do?" his question, "What's your story?" opened my heart valve a quarter turn so the true waters could flow.

Adam knows his actor friends are often embarrassed by discussing their day jobs when they'd rather be acting full-time, so instead he asks, "What's your passion?" Another friend once asked me, "So what'd you do in your pre-kid life?" Some people ask a question similar to Adam's friend: "What's your life story?" And there is always the easy add-on: "Tell me more."

Surely unearthing people's stories is the cornerstone of hospitality. Do I make space for people to share their stories? What makes a person tick, turn, or tumble, spinning them forward, backward, or sideways? What passions propel a person into motion? Assuming that curiosity and questions are welcome, do I have the time to dig a bit deeper into someone else's story? Do I allow others access to mine?

* * *

Our schedules and tasks often barricade us from the intimacy and community we desire. Lack of time can make prioritizing people or bumping into acquaintances more of an annoyance than a gift.

On our first visit to Fort Collins, I had noticed many aspen trees and weeping willows clustered together around a creek that roamed through the entire city and a bike path that ran alongside it. Colorado labels these areas "open spaces." Chicago, too, has a vast amount of land designated for recreation. Some call it waste, as this is land that might be sold as prime real estate. But despite the monetary value, someone in government made the wise choice to set aside open land for nature, play, and rest. What if we retained space in our lives— like the land carved out from Colorado's ranches, subdivisions, and cities to be protected as recreational "open space"—and reserved it for relationships and wonder?

A month before traveling to Uganda, I had sipped chai in a Kenyan friend's off-campus apartment. I wanted to get to know some African women before I left. "It's been difficult to find friends here in the Midwest," she lamented. "In my culture, we just drop by one another's homes unannounced. I've learned the hard way that you can't do that here in America." I knew what she meant. That year I was a resident assistant on a floor for first-year students, and I found that even in our dormitory, the students preferred to send messages via computer rather than walk down the hallway to chat face-to-face.

When I moved to Uganda just a few months later, I realized that going to and from work with my host mother easily took twice as long as it "should" have taken because of all the greetings exchanged along the way. When my Ugandan friends went visiting, they would call out, "I'm going benching!" Or when a visitor arrived, "Rita, your bencher's here!" The "bencher" was often someone of the opposite sex, but benching also meant going around visiting friends. No one called ahead, but the bencher was rarely turned away. In the West, we don't often appreciate surprise visitors, and we plan far into the future. But perhaps we need to relearn the art of stopping by.

American missionary friends living in Tajikistan confessed to mustering up the courage to spontaneously drop by homes to forge new friendships in their context. In much of the world, visiting is a daily pastime. In her book *The Village Effect*, Susan Pinker writes that "daily face-to-face contact with a tight group of friends and family helps you live longer." She confessed that researching for her book altered her own social habits, and she admits that "now I build in social contact the way I build in daily exercise."[5]

Through her research, Pinker discovered that in certain remote villages on the Italian island of Sardinia, there are, proportionally, six to ten times as many people who live past the age of one hundred as in modern cities around the world.[6] She was shocked when she discovered why. Pinker said it's not necessarily because they exercise, have healthy eating habits, or don't smoke. Instead, research indicates it's because they live in a tight-knit community and have frequent face-to-face interactions.

According to a study by psychologist Julianne Holt-Lunstad, the close relationships we have and number of social interactions we maintain throughout the day, called "social integration," can indeed influence our longevity.[7] Another study found that "getting to know one's neighbors can help reduce loneliness. Thirty-three percent of midlife and older adults who have ever spoken to their neighbors are lonely, compared with 61 percent who have *never* spoken to a neighbor."[8]

Sometimes it's easier to slow down and admire a sunset than it is to stop and talk to a neighbor. How many people outside our families know what's going on in the interior rooms of our hearts? Are we in a daily routine that leads us to see the same people every day or at least every week? Who would be the first ones to notice our tear-stained faces after the loss of a loved one, a breakup, or a devastating phone call? Would they sense that something was wrong because they see us so many of the other days? I don't need to be close to everyone, but my soul longs for a slightly wider and deeper circle of intimacy.

Jesus never considered people to be interruptions. Luke 8:43-48 tells the story of a woman who had been bleeding for twelve years creeping through the crowd. Kneeling down, she reached her hand around swishing robes and dirty feet just to touch the fabric of Jesus' clothing. Jesus had just stopped a raging storm on the sea, then cast demons out of a madman, and was on his way to help a dying little girl. If anyone could claim to be busy, Jesus could. Yet when he felt the woman's hand reach out and touch him, he paused what he was doing and directed all his attention to her. This seemingly insignificant decision to stop came at a cost. The delay meant a little girl died of illness; but a chronically bleeding woman was healed.

Sometimes I think Jesus liked to dillydally. He slept on a boat through a storm as the disciples panicked (Mark 4:38-40). He told his followers to be like the flowers of the field and the birds of the air—unconcerned with how their physical needs would be met (Matthew 6:26-40). Jesus took his time—noticing fig trees, lepers, men in sycamore trees, and grubby children hugging his knees (Mark 11:12-25; Matthew 8:1-4; Luke 19:1-10; Matthew 18:2-6). Jesus was not in a hurry to *do*. He believed God could work miracles through him *being* who he was made to be.

* * *

When I lived in China, I stumbled on many cultural differences relating to time. My Chinese students usually stood me up. At least at first. Part of my job description in China as a missionary-who-wasn't-allowed-to-call-herself-a-missionary included building relationships. This translated to hours of waiting for students by the school gate to go out for meals at hole-in-the-wall noodle restaurants. For the first month, I often stood at the gate alone. I stared quizzically at my flip phone and mulled over what I had done wrong.

After a few weeks, I realized my problem: I was scheduling meals too far in advance. Coming from the United States, I planned appointments about a week or two out. But after being stood up over and over again, I had a growing hunch my students weren't writing down appointments in calendars at all. (In fact, I doubted they even *owned* calendars.) I proved my theory once during an American and British culture class when I sketched the days of the week with chalk across the blackboard, putting a star under "Sunday."

"If you wanted to invite me for a meal on Sunday," I asked the class, "which day would you text or call to ask me?" The class of forty students decided they'd ask either on Saturday (the day before) or on Sunday (the day of). They gasped when I revealed that in the United States, we often ask a week or more in advance. (I didn't tell them that some people schedule six or more weeks out.)

So during my next four years in China, I still planned meals with students in my paper calendar, but I wouldn't invite them until the day before. The meeting had been on my calendar for more than a week, but they didn't know it. That way, if something else came up for me to do, my schedule flexed with ambiguity—because I hadn't actually asked them yet.

In the United States and much of the West, time is a commodity. We talk about time the way we talk about money: we waste time, spend time, save time, make time, run out of time, and keep time. The Bible says our hearts reside where we place our treasure (Matthew 6:21). Perhaps we worship the commodity of time as our greatest treasure.

Not all Westerners are overscheduled or frustrated by interruptions. The pastor of one of the churches we visited confessed in a sermon about partnering with another predominantly white church and the local (and only) black church in town to host a visiting college gospel choir. The African

American pastor of the black church sent an email to my pastor and the other pastor saying he'd have dinner available at his church for the gospel choir at three o'clock. The white pastors decided that five in the evening was plenty of time for the choir to eat before the seven o'clock concert, so they invited the choir to arrive later in the day.

"I felt very disrespected when you made that decision," the African American pastor later told the men. "In our church, we value relationship over time. That would have been an excellent opportunity to hang out over food and spend time with those college students."

Whether we are spontaneous or stay in our structured Google Calendar boxes, many of us in the West tend to be more scheduled and task-oriented than most of the rest of the world. Perhaps we need to start planning to be spontaneous. One online friend who lives abroad said she purposely plans only one commitment a week so she can leave the rest of her days free for spontaneous hospitality. We can keep drinks in our fridge and chocolate chip cookies and lasagna in our freezer to warm in the microwave for unexpected guests. We can save a few nights here and there to be "spontaneous."

* * *

We left Mr. Sunde and his shop at ten thirty that night. We stumbled out to the street as if under a charm. On the drive home, Adam and I agreed we wouldn't be surprised if we drove up the next day to find a Verizon store or a vacant retail space in place of the mysterious museum.

What if we hadn't meandered into the shop? What if instead of lingering and talking, we had rushed off to our next event? Life would have gone on, but we would have missed a little bit of whimsy and a lot of wonder. I hoped to always be able to build time into my days to stop and chat not just with a neighbor but with a complete stranger.

If time is our treasure, how can we worship God and honor one another with it? Like my Ugandan friends, how can I make socializing a natural part of my life? I hope to set my schedule by people instead of by tasks. People are eternal; the dishes, laundry, lawn, and football game are not. In *An Altar in the World*, Barbara Brown Taylor says, "The practice of paying attention is as simple as looking twice at the people and things you might just as easily ignore. To see takes time, like having a friend takes time. It is as simple as turning off the television to learn the song of a single bird."[9]

Even the song of a lark.

*Acquaintance without patience is like
a candle with no light.*

—Iranian proverb

FIVE

The Friendship Conundrum

college classmate once accused me of being a friend collector. I would have taken it as a compliment, except she sneered as she said it. It's true. I used to gather friends the way my daughter collects wildflowers in the spring, clumping them together in every fist, pocket, and buttonhole. But I've had less gusto for forging friendships in my thirties. I've lost the zest and zeal for developing new relationships because it seems like either I or the other person will move away. Tilling tired soil feels futile. Yet loneliness motivates me to keep trying. Deep down, I know that God-sparks fly when we sync with other souls earmarked for the eternal.

Having lived in the city of Chicago (not the suburbs—a very important distinction for Chicagoans) and overseas in Uganda and China, I can get snobby about people I meet. I assume everyone is boring until proven otherwise. Suspicious, I wave my butterfly net, trying to catch a new flying friend who might be edgy, weird, alluring, countercultural, or exotic on some level. Would they make a good addition to my friend collection?

* * *

The older I get, the less I know where to start with new people. How much history do I need to divulge before I feel known? Which questions should I ask to unlock the hidden rooms in the hearts of those I meet? Our layers are buried deep, but we feel they are a part of us and essential to belonging.

My aunt gives gifts in the form of a "birthday ball." She begins with a small item and wraps it in crepe paper until it's completely covered. Then she adds another small object and wraps that gift as well. She continues this process until the sphere is about the size of a basketball and conceals at least ten different gifts. We are all birthday balls: bound-up histories hidden beneath each new layer of life that overlays it. Most levels lie dormant, although our oldest friends know the former versions of us. As each year swaths us with yet another layer, we wonder how new friends will know the true us without knowing all that lies beneath the surface.

After their retirement, my parents traded flip-flops for snow skis and swimsuits for long underwear to move from Tampa, Florida, to a home nine thousand feet above sea level and three hours from us in the Colorado Rockies. One clear winter day I snowshoed with my mom, the cobalt sky a backdrop to the aspen and spruce trees standing watch over us. She told me about the elk and moose they had spotted recently. I told her about my disdain for playdates with shrieking children and disjointed conversation, and I admitted that finding friends had been challenging since our move.

"How do you begin new friendships at age sixty-four?" I asked her. "Don't you want new friends to know your history? Where do you start?" We stepped around the fallen pine trees that littered the ground like oversized pickup sticks.

She paused, her snowshoes sinking into drifts of snow, then answered, "I start from now."

My mom has learned what I am still beginning to grasp. We are not a chapter or a single experience or a particular identity. We are a composite. All our past experiences intertwine into one exquisite design the longer we live. And while we know that God has walked with us on every road along the way, not every person we encounter needs to know each bend in our journey. There's a beauty in the secret paths we've traversed—a whispering between Jesus and us.

We start from now.

* * *

I am a hopeless Bible study dropout. Since beginning to have children, I can't seem to commit to any group I join. Our second year in Colorado, I pulled up my chair to the circle of my newest group—one of about fifty groups meeting in the same building—and sized up the collection of Colorado women.

Snap judgments flashed in my mind, summing up each woman at a glance: Pretty. Perfect. Sheltered. Shallow. Boring. Boring. Boring.

"Okay," the leader started, clearing her throat. "I was thinking we could introduce ourselves this first class. If you wouldn't mind, could you tell us a little about yourselves?"

I inwardly debated which image of myself I wanted to convey in less than two minutes. Which layer should I divulge to this group of strange women? Which 0.001 percent of my life should I share? I went first, saying I was married with three kids (mothers always share these things first, I've noticed), a writer, and used to teach middle school. I patted myself on the back for not mentioning I had lived in China for five years just to prove how interesting I was.

The women began sharing, introducing the most imperative details of their twenty, thirty, or forty years of life, distilled into a few sentences.

"I lived in Jerusalem for five years."

"My husband and I tour the country in a trailer with a group of orphans from Africa who perform at different churches, so I'll be gone a lot."

"My husband died in a car accident two years ago on our way to deliver our third child and I'm getting remarried in October. Combined, we'll have seven kids."

"I got pregnant when I was nineteen, but got married a few years after that."

"My husband and I work with international students at the university. We lived in Indonesia for six years."

I was stunned. All it took was for one woman to open her mouth to remind me that each one had a unique and fascinating story—even the ones who hadn't traveled, earned degrees, or had unusual twists and turns in life.

When the group discussion ended, I followed the stream of women down the hall toward the sanctuary for the lecture part of the morning. I tried to make small talk with a few as we trickled through the hallway, skipping going to the bathroom since I knew that would leave me sitting by myself in the auditorium during the lecture. Settling into wooden pews, we thumbed through the hymnals until we reached the correct page number, then stood, a group of hundreds of women singing in unison.

I glanced past the hymnal, distracted by the three-story-tall stained glass window at the front of the church. The window had black lines swooping through a kaleidoscope of colored glass fragments. It was as if a queen had dashed her crown of gems to the ground and an artist had meticulously pieced together the shards. The lower half had less vibrant colors, while the patterns above mingled with sunbeams to sing brilliance to boring. This grand mosaic whispered about the mystery of human beings and the paradox of being both broken and beautiful, messy and multifaceted, fragile and fierce. Alone, the pieces were broken glass. Together, they were dazzling.

* * *

All the social "shoulds" of friendship can sometimes feel overwhelming. Currently, I have several hundred Facebook friends, and am active on Instagram, Twitter, and Pinterest. As a writer, I add a "friend" almost daily. Meanwhile, I've had a tough time staying in contact with friends from the past. While social media helps us feel seen, heard, and connected, and while it truly *can* lead to lifelong friendships, it also adds relationships we have no time or energy to maintain.

When I feel ashamed about not keeping up with friendships, I thumb back through Anne Morrow Lindbergh's *Gift from the Sea*. She talks about the pressure on women to be the "hub of the wheel." Although the book was written in 1955, it could easily have been written today. Lindbergh writes, "For life today in America is based on the premise of ever-widening circles of contact and communication. It involves not only family demands, but community demands, national demands, international demands on the good citizen, through social and cultural pressures, through newspapers, magazines, radio programs, political drives, charitable appeals and so on. My mind reels with it. What a circus act we women perform every day of our lives."[1]

No wonder practicing hospitality feels impossible. Those of us who are parents to small children often congratulate ourselves on just showering and overseeing the personal hygiene of the people who live under our roof, with bonus points for taking family pictures, sending Christmas cards, or writing thank you notes. As the hub of the wheel, we can find ourselves spinning out of control of our schedule and time, not to mention the hospitality and relationships we once planned to prioritize.

Malcolm Gladwell discusses the idea that humans can only maintain about 150 relationships, and even fewer than that can fit on our "sympathy list": the list of people we know intimately, which includes about twelve people.[2] Gladwell reports British anthropologist Robin Dunbar's findings on the frequency of the number 150 in anthropological literature.[3] Hunter-gatherer societies, religious colonies, self-sufficient agricultural collectives all usually topped off at the number 150.

Jesus had three close friends; nine additional disciples; other friends not considered "disciples," like Mary, Martha, Zacchaeus, and Lazarus; social misfit friends; and then crowds of people after that. But if Jesus was not intimate with every person in his circle, then we shouldn't feel burdened to maintain intimacy with every Facebook friend and acquaintance.

* * *

Adam and I each held an edge of the sheet, and it billowed and ballooned in rebellion of lying flat and smooth as we raised and lowered it. Static snapped in the dry Colorado air.

"I'm kind of nervous," Adam admitted, pulling down the corner of the sheet, wrestling the material into compliance.

"Me too," I said. "I'm overcompensating by buying so much food."

The night the Iranian family arrived, I spent the evening stocking the mini fridge in their bedroom with cheese, apples, orange juice, water, and yogurt. The bathroom was clean, the sheets fresh, and the carpet vacuumed. We jerry-rigged a curtain on a tension rod at the top of the basement stairs to give the semblance of privacy. Adam had studied up on how to say hello in Persian, and I had made a last trip to the grocery store to stock up on the basics. The kitchen fridge looked like we were bracing for a blizzard rather than hosting guests for five nights.

For the past year I had been attending the International Women's Club with women from India, Indonesia, China, Turkey, Sri Lanka, and many other places. We met in an outdated rec room of the apartment complex where many of the international student families lived. The American women who attended had all either traveled, adopted non-American children, or lived abroad. As returned American expats or those with connections to other countries, we shared the common culture of fitting in everywhere and nowhere. We had learned other languages, altered our Western ways to assimilate to new ways of doing simple tasks like cleaning, cooking, and even using the bathroom. Now we were back in our "home" culture of the United States, but internally we felt homeless.

I invited some of the women to my home for brunch before Christmas. I overheard Maggie, the home-stay coordinator, telling another woman she was having a hard time finding a host for a family of four from Iran coming a couple of weeks before Christmas. The husband would be a visiting scholar at the university. They only needed a place for five nights, but most host homes could accommodate singles, not entire families.

"We have a spare room we haven't been able to rent out yet if you need it," I offered. "And they could use the space in the basement too."

"That'd be great," she said. "Would you be ready for them to come next week?"

* * *

The doorbell rang and I stumbled off the couch, smoothed my hair, and slid on my slippers. I glanced at the clock. It was a quarter after eleven in the evening. I had fallen asleep. Adam closed his book and we rushed to the door and opened it to a man, a woman, a girl, a boy, and their driver, who told us he was from the university.

Rahim was about the height of Adam, but probably ten years older, with silver and black hair, bushy eyebrows, and a kind smile. Behind him was his wife, Azita, who looked about my age. She smiled, pushing back her caramel hair. She wore salmon-colored pants and an aqua sweater with a silver cat on it. Although I gestured that they should come inside, she turned to stone, her children cowering behind her, their frightened black eyes peering from either side of their mother. Months later when I thought of their arrival, I mostly thought of those huge dark eyes. After traveling more than thirty hours to a new country where they couldn't understand the words the strangers were speaking at them, they must have been terrified.

"Come in, come in," I said. "You're welcome here. Come inside!" They still didn't move. What was I doing wrong? What could I say to get them to come inside? I finally grabbed Azita's arm and gently pulled her through the door. She said something to the children, and they walked behind her, dragging their feet and bowing their heads.

"Should we take off our shoes?" Rahim asked.

"You don't need to," I said. "Just do what's most comfortable for you."

At this, the two-year-old girl sat on the bottom step by the front door and wailed. I looked at Rahim, questioningly.

"She wants to take her shoes off," he said, looking down at his little girl, who had finally fallen apart after days of travel.

"Oh! Then she can take her shoes off! Whatever's best for you. I know you've had a very long journey and must be so tired. You can just head downstairs and sleep if you want."

"Yes, thank you," Rahim said.

Azita nodded at me, smiling. "Thank you," she said, helping her daughter take off her hot pink shoes.

Although they mostly slept off their jetlag during their stay with us, we took turns cooking for each other when we could. We learned that Rahim had come to the United States to study basil seeds for a year, and Azita had a degree in entomology. We chuckled as Rahim discovered his love for the children's book about Frog and Toad, and we snapped pictures of him reading to all the children. After five nights in our home, they were able to move to their apartment complex in the university apartments. I missed them when they moved across town.

"You should come visit me," Azita said one day after they had invited us over for dinner at their new apartment. "We could sit and talk while the kids play."

I visited them many times, marveling as I watched their small, bare apartment transform into a home. Their son learned English after spending just six months in an American kindergarten; and their daughter eventually attended an American preschool where Azita volunteered. Mostly, I was awed by their hospitality, which I both experienced and watched them extend to others around them.

* * *

I was visiting Azita when an Iranian friend of hers, Mary, stopped by to chat. We snacked on dates dipped in honey and drank grapefruit juice out of ceramic mugs. We attempted to talk as our children played and argued, played and argued some more. Mary had lived in the apartment complex for eight years while her husband was getting his PhD, and she told me how she loved the community there. After Mary left, Azita and I wrestled shoes onto the kids and strolled down the sidewalk to the apartment playground. The kids sprinted ahead through the high spring grass. Azita and I chatted about her life back in Iran, our husbands, and the monotony, mayhem, and hilarity of life with little children. We had nothing in common, and we had everything in common.

After the kids played at the playground, Azita, the kids, and I returned to her house to eat lentils stewed in tomatoes and onions over rice. I glanced at the clock and said I needed to return home because Adam would be home from work soon. Loading the kids into the car and then backing out of the parking lot, I tuned out the kids' chatter and sank into my thoughts.

I loved spending time with Azita, Rahim, and their kids, Faraz and Sara, but was I setting myself up for loneliness when they left in a few months? After years of making friends only to say goodbye, could I continue with yet another friendship with an expiration date? Was it worth it?

* * *

Two years before I met Azita, during our first summer in Colorado, I schlepped our two kids to a church for the weekly women's book study. The flyer posted in the church foyer said they planned to discuss a book on female friendship. The cover—with two pretty women in oversized, comfy shirts having a heart-to-heart—looked so cheesy I almost didn't join the book study. But I was desperate for contact with adults and free childcare during the scorching summer months, so I overlooked the seemingly fluffy topic.

I joined white-haired women and a few other frazzled moms around a table in the baby blue Sunday school classroom in the church basement. Rancher women shared prayer requests involving cattle and broken fences, and I chuckled inwardly at the otherworldliness of our move from Chicago to Colorado.

In the book, the author pointed out the value of both perennial and annual friendships. (As a new gardener, it seems like I have to look those terms up again every gardening season to remember which is which.) She said some friendships are perennial—long-term—while some are like annuals, lasting only for a season. Her point was that even temporary friendships are worth cultivating.[4]

But why? I thought. What's the point in trying when your friendship investment will move to another place? When we had lived in Chicago, a friend who attended our very transient church admitted as much to me. "I didn't bother getting to know her," she once said to me about another woman, "because she told me she planned on moving to Michigan eventually." I was careful not to mention to that friend that we, too, were most likely going to move away soon.

One of the glitches in being a goer is that you tend to forge friendships with other goers. That first summer in Colorado, I geared up to start "friend dating," which sometimes required me to give my phone number to random women. I met Kat at the park when our sons chased one another and hugged goodbye so tightly that they fell to the ground in a giggling heap. We both had little girls in baby carriers with chubby legs dangling from our chests, and I said, "I never do this, but can I give you my phone number? We should get together at a park again sometime." She laughed and agreed.

We hung out almost weekly at parks, pools, and museums. Our boys chased, jumped, and wrestled, and our girls, just three months apart, navigated toddlerhood in tandem, learning to teeter, climb, and eventually run together. I discovered Kat not only was an artist but also owned a martial arts school with her husband. Some google stalking early on uncovered that she was a champion mixed martial arts fighter. Her laid-back parenting style helped me learn to ease up on my kids and encourage them to delve into imaginative play.

About a year later, I also got to know my neighbor Jess. She had a four-year-old boy and invited us over every week so the boys could race Hot Wheels around on the carpet or build skyscrapers out of Legos. She adored her kids. Being with her, I grew in gratitude for this stage of my own children's lives too.

Both Kat and Jess entertained thoughts of leaving our area—of moving to Hawaii or Spain, Alaska or South America. After months of listening to both of them brainstorm about relocating, I stopped believing they would act. So I was shocked when they both decided to go—Kat to Austin and Jess to Seattle. Within six months, my two closest friends in my new city were gone.

* * *

Swiss psychologist Carl Jung, who founded analytical psychology, wrote that "the meeting of two personalities is like the contact of two chemical substances: if there is any reaction, both are transformed."[5] He used this to prove that psychologists themselves are transformed by their relationships with their patients. Sharing space with Kat and Jess for the short time I knew them changed me. I drew life from them and they from me. It was a loss to have them leave.

When my husband, Adam, was a kid, he used to hide cups of apple juice in the Sunday school cabinets at church and then return each week to see if anything had grown. He still loves science experiments, apparently, because these days he hides a brown, bubbly liquid in our kitchen cabinet in an attempt to grow a sourdough starter. He begins with whole wheat flour and water, then adds half a cup more each day to feed the yeast.

"Where does the yeast come from, anyway?" I asked, accidentally smearing jelly into the kitchen counter in an attempt to wipe it clean.

"It comes from the air," he said. "So this dough will be special Colorado bread, while other bread made, say, in California will have some of the elements of California air in it. Isn't that cool?" I gave him a you're-such-a-nerd-but-I-love-you-because-of-it smirk.

"So do you need to make a new starter with each new loaf of bread?" I said, putting the sponge back in the sink.

"No, once you do this, you can use part, then keep the rest and keep feeding it to use later."

Stacking the last of the dishes in the dishwasher, I thought about the bubbling dough breathing and gobbling up invisible airborne yeast from inside the kitchen cabinet. I hoped it wouldn't grow mold or stink up the room. Yet it reminded me of the magic of God—the miracle of a transformed soul, multiplied loaves and fish for a crowd, and a flaming bush that burned without being consumed. It made me think of the kingdom of God and the humble beginnings for powerful, yet invisible, movements of God in the world. And it reminded me that just because we give a part of ourselves to someone in an offer of friendship doesn't mean we're used up.

The air of a particular place we breathe, the pH of the warm soil we wiggle into, and the people we meet: all these feed and change us at an elemental level. We keep growing, if only to be torn and offered to the next human soul we encounter at the park, in the next cubicle over, walking outside with a stroller, at the local book club, or while eating bagels together after church. "Make room for us in your hearts," the apostle Paul said to the Corinthians (2 Corinthians 7:2). In the economy of God, parts of ourselves are torn away to create new friendships, but we stay alive. God repropagates the parts that are lost because we gave them away to an international student, to a family member who passed away, or to a friend who moved across the country. God's love is the starter that can never die but lives on even as it is given away. God regenerates us with the Spirit's power so we can keep nourishing one another with our presence.

Where one eats, two can eat.

—**Colombian proverb**

SIX

Habits of Hospitality

Stirring the bubbling spaghetti sauce from a jar, I felt a twinge of guilt about serving my family comfort food so often recently. Darkness pooled in corners of the house long before dinner, and sleep tugged on all of us. As we neared the winter solstice, the temptation was strong to dive into full-on hibernation mode. The last thing I wanted was to invite someone over to my home.

My friend Jess had moved away the week before, and I loathed the idea of risking relationship again. I thought of the Bible verse I'd loved during my first year of college: "Enlarge the place of your tent, stretch your tent curtains wide, do not hold back; lengthen your cords, strengthen your stakes" (Isaiah 54:2). These days, I wanted to shrink back, pull up my cords, and wrap my tent tightly around myself. I didn't want a wide tent; I was happy with my small one. I wanted to dive under warm blankets, not wipe my counters or prepare food for a crowd. Yet I kept coming back to a single word.

Invite.

That morning I had shivered in the chill before the kids' small heels thudded on the wooden floors above. In the quiet, I meditated on words scrawled in black ink on an index card. "Blessed are those who are invited to the wedding supper of the Lamb!" (Revelation 19:9). I closed my eyes, imagining.

I inhaled the words: *Blessed. Invited. Wedding supper. Lamb.* Each word punctured the tight walls threatening to cave in on me.

I offered every restriction back as an exhale: *Busyness. Time. Schedule. Noise. Mess. Chaos. Inconvenience. Control. Insecurity. Rejection. Fear.* There were so many reasons not to invite, so many walls rising to keep me shut in, alone, and lonely. But God reminded me why I invite at all.

You are invited, God seemed to whisper.

Jesus persistently invites us to his sacred space. Jesus drags a chair to his table, then urges us to sit. He invites us no matter where we've been, what we're wearing, whom we're with, or what amount of luggage we bring to the room. He speaks our name. He chose that name before we were in our mother's womb. He asks us to explore more rooms in his house, enjoy a feast at his table, and drench ourselves in his Spirit, who has flooded the room.

Come in, Rabbi Jesus says. *Sit next to me. Be my confidant. Lean on my chest. Sit at my feet. Hold my secrets. Shrug on my shawl of joy. Now look around. See him? See her? Love them too. I put them next to you in life so you would invite them to share this table.*

You are invited.

Now invite.

* * *

In the fall of my junior year of high school, my mom and I visited a potential college and stayed in a campus apartment with Melanie, a sophomore someone from church had connected us with. We sat sipping chamomile tea on the couch as my mom asked Melanie about classes and extracurriculars at the school.

"So what do you think you want to do after you graduate?" my mom asked, making small talk. Melanie's answer was so strange, I still remember it to this day.

"I want to have an 'open home,'" she said.

What twenty-year-old says that? I thought. Most are charting careers, and some are hoping they'll bump serendipitously into the love of their lives at the cafeteria cereal bar. Most desire to soak up every opportunity offered in college and want to push the boundaries of independence.

But I absorbed Melanie's curious dream into my own life mission as I jumped into college life and then early adulthood, living with roommates in Chicago, teaching in China, and finally writing and parenting back in the United States. In Chicago, an open home looked like spontaneously inviting friends over and, when more people showed up than expected, marveling at the magic of bottomless tortilla soup. In China, it looked like middle school kids knocking on my door on the weekends to practice English, or twenty students squeezing into my three-hundred-square-foot apartment. At my current stage of life, having an open home looks like doors forgetfully flung wide and plastic pools of shiny, slippery children. It looks like parents arriving at dinnertime to retrieve little ones and chatting with us at the kitchen island as I chop cilantro, lime, and onions. Whatever season of life—whether with wide or narrow tent walls—I want an open home.

* * *

My neighbor Holly texted me one hot summer morning the year after we moved to our new house in Colorado: "Can I come over and we'll hang out in your driveway while the kids play out front this afternoon?"

"Sure!" I responded, making a mental note to pop some popcorn to bring outside.

My next-door neighbor Jim usually did the driveway hosting. He kept a keg in his garage, and the neighbors sat sipping Bud Lite from red Solo cups, a few of them smoking and smashing their cigarette butts into an old Folgers canister. Jim and Bonnie had been out of town for the week, leaving a void on our street. I rarely hung out with the driveway-sitters, mainly because most either were retired or had older kids who could be left alone for more than three minutes at a time. My kids would eat dinner at four thirty if I let them, so I was usually preparing food while the socializing happened.

Holly arrived at five o'clock, and I dragged the lawn chairs out and arranged them under the canopy of trees in our driveway. I heard a scraping sound and turned to see Elijah and Adeline heaving their child-sized camping chairs from the back to the front yard. They had every intention of crashing our mom party.

Soon after Holly and I sat down, our neighbor Jim, returned from out of town, pulled up in his pickup truck. Noticing our small gathering, he joined us. Slowly, others trickled over— Jim's wife, Bonnie, Holly's husband, Peter, and a retired couple from down the street. I glanced at my phone. It was six o'clock.

We usually ate dinner around six, so I was conflicted. End the impromptu party, or think of a quick dinner plan?

I whispered to Adam to go inside to start the rice cooker. Beans and rice would be easy. I handed him the key to the house. I had a clean house for once, so I had locked all the doors so the kids couldn't destroy it while the adults chatted outside. Does this still qualify as an open home? I thought. Another inner voice countered: Limits are okay. This, too, is hospitality.

A woman I hadn't met before arrived, and Peter ran over to Jim's house to pull over another lawn chair. Clearly I wasn't prepared for the masses. Holly leaned over her phone, and I wondered who she was texting. After a couple of minutes, she whispered with a wink, "Pizza is on its way."

Adam set up a folding table in the driveway for the pizza boxes and I ran inside to grab paper plates, napkins, and a water pitcher. We ate pizza off paper plates propped on our laps, talking and laughing. The sun eased behind the trees, slicing lines of light across the pavement. Adam scooped up Isaiah to put him to bed, and a little later, I took the older two up to their bunk beds upstairs. The pop-up party lasted until after nine, when the darkness drove everyone back to their houses.

I wish I could always be as flexible, relaxed, and spontaneous as I was that night to hold space for surprise soul-feeding parties connecting me to my neighbors. But time. Dinners. Bedtimes. Deadlines. Moods. I've heard grandmas tell new moms to follow nap schedules for kids most of the time so they can skip naps on other days. Perhaps we need this sort of moderation in our social lives—we usually stick to our bedtimes, deadlines, and schedules so we can splurge on people when community parks out in our driveway.

* * *

Inviting others into our home and life splits open a larger work of God in the world. Like the Israelites who dipped their toes in the current before God piled the waters into a heap for them to cross (Joshua 3:14-17), our responsibility is to make the first move and ask. Or in the case of my friend Holly inviting herself over, we simply say yes to an invitation. And after we ask someone into our lives, God hauls other obstacles out of our way one by one. God pulls up our perfectionism, limited resources, pride, insecurities, reservations, awkwardness, and loneliness and clears the way for us to relate to one another on solid ground.

Hospitality is not for the called or gifted. It's not for the gregarious extroverts with huge houses and overflowing bank accounts. And it's not for the people with angelic children, respectable roommates, or perfect marriages. Contrary to those spiritual gift tests that catalog hospitality as a special talent, nowhere in the Bible is it named as such. Instead, hospitality is a command (see Romans 12:13; 1 Peter 4:9). Hospitality is for everyone.

Creative hospitality morphs to adapt to our ages, stages, and strengths in life. Often, we're already showing hospitality in ways that feel natural to us. Some of us may become "front yard people," like Kristin Schell of *The Turquoise Table*, and place a picnic table, chairs, or swing in the front yard and invite neighbors to come.[1] This can look like planting our thyme and rosemary in the front yard instead of the back, or drinking coffee in lawn chairs on our driveways or front stoops instead of our private patios or living rooms. When we lived in an apartment in Chicago and Elijah was a toddler, we spent late afternoons in the summer wandering the sidewalk up and down our street.

My friend Sarah, who lives in Michigan, organizes the moms on her street to walk together one morning a week. She also invites all her kids' same-gender classmates over to her home four times over the course of the school year. As a full-time nurse, she can't volunteer at her kids' public school often, but she can plan a few activities and buy snacks for the kids and parents to come to her.

We can develop a lifestyle of hospitality by hosting block parties, Christmas open houses, or summer cookouts for our neighbors. Those in apartments can invite neighbors to come for a party or dinner; and those with small homes need only pull up an extra chair to invite a college student or single person to their table. Hospitality can look like going out after work with our coworkers or inviting our colleagues into our homes for a meal. One of my friends invites her children's public school principal over for dinner each year—we could ask their teachers too.

Tracy Johnson, founder of the blog *Red Tent Living*, felt compelled to invite twelve women to her home. She passed around a basket of random objects and asked each woman to use one prop to tell a story about her life. They sat around that table for more than three hours, sharing stories together. She asked if they'd want to meet again, and they enthusiastically agreed. She handed each one a red rose on the way out, saying the rose was their prompt for next month. The format eventually rounded off at nine months and the number of women trimmed down to six or eight, but this began a movement of women meeting together to tell their stories. Tracy had no idea how it would all play out in the end; she only knew she needed to invite women to gather. She invited twelve, and everyone said yes.[2] She *invited*.

Sometimes we can be tempted to leave church when we feel unseen. But what if we took a new approach? A tiny book on hospitality called *The Hospitality Commands* by Alexander Strauch tells a story of a couple who, instead of leaving the church where they felt lonely and disconnected, made the conscious decision to invite a new person or family over every single week. At the end of the year, strangers had become guests and guests had become friends. They reaped what they sowed.[3] What if instead of waiting for an invitation, we asked first?

My church while I was in college had an "adopt a college student" program. Nearly every Sunday, I ate lunch with Sharon, Mark and their four children, ages three, five, seven, and nine. Sharon crafted yeast rolls from scratch, roasted chicken, and created midwestern Jell-O "salads" loaded with mini marshmallows, chopped pecans, and grapes. After lunch, the older children loaded the dishwasher and Mark brewed fresh coffee. The kids listened to my romantic woes as I schemed with Mark and Sharon over coffee in their den, talking into the tired afternoon.

My parents lived one thousand miles away in Florida, but this family welcomed me, a stranger. Now that I have tiny children of my own, I can imagine the strain of hosting every single week. I'm not sure I could do it. It didn't occur to me that I might be inconveniencing Sharon and Mark, slicing into their family time or sabotaging their Sunday afternoon naps. They welcomed me without hesitation or fanfare, their actions demonstrating I belonged and was worthy of their attention.

When our biological families live far away, our neighbors, friends, and church members can become stand-in family.

Retirees can bless families with young children by becoming honorary grandmas and grandpas. They can share their wisdom and stories with those younger than them or apprentice new homeowners, parents, gardeners, seamstresses, or cooks. Families can invite single people, widows, and retirees to join their chaos and become adopted aunts and uncles to their children.

Going on retreats, camping trips, or vacations together as a group accelerates friendships. There's something about waking up in the morning and having a person see you in all your bed-headed, coffeeless glory to propel you from acquaintance to friend. Personally, I think we need more (G-rated) adult sleepovers.

Reimagining hospitality in the West requires cavorting with a God who delights in busting up our normalcy with divine creativity. Loving strangers, opening our homes, inviting others, accepting invitations, and sometimes inviting ourselves into a person's life are all habits that huddle together under the umbrella of hospitality.

* * *

Sometimes we invite people into what we're already doing. We can invite others to love what we love, do what we do, and go where we go. The premise of the book *Family on Mission* suggests that we stop compartmentalizing our "ministries" and invite people into our everyday lives.[4] Many churches sling around terms like *missional living, living on mission,* and *holistic ministry.* We don't need more programs or plans for living missionally in the world; we just need to invite others to walk with us in our right-now life. We're already cooking dinner, so why not invite someone to join us? We're already taking our family to the pool. Why not ask that neighbor family to come along too?

We had barely seen the parents of our international student renter Priya, even though they had been with us for a full week. We were up before six and usually out of the house by nine to go to work, preschool, or other activities. Priya and her family ate breakfast at nine thirty, lunch at two thirty, and dinner at nine, so our meals didn't line up. After experiencing extravagant hospitality when I lived in China, Tajikistan, and Uganda, I felt guilty that I couldn't show our Indian guests the hospitality I knew they were used to experiencing. I wasn't preparing elaborate meals, feeding them at all times of the day, or playing tour guide for them.

"Would you like to come to a nature area with us?" I finally asked. They had encouraged the kids to call them Baba and Aayi, Father and Mother.

"Yes, yes, we will come," Baba said, smiling, his head moving side to side in rhythm with his words.

Elijah shifted his booster seat to the back of the car, and I swept aside the preschool crafts, sunglasses, and empty coffee cups to make room for them in the minivan. Aayi sat silently in front with me while Baba sat in the back and played peekaboo with Isaiah, with Elijah and Adeline poking him from behind. After ten minutes, I pulled into the gravel parking lot and pointed to the tree-lined ponds sparkling in the sunshine.

"We're here," I said.

Isaiah held my finger as we led the way down the path between two ponds. Baba and Aayi idled behind as Elijah and Adeline terrorized us by running to the edge of the water, then stopping abruptly to peer into the pond.

"Come here, come here," Baba gestured, indicating they should come closer to the path. They ignored him, tossing sticks into the clear water and squatting on the bank to jab at ants. We rounded the first pond and walked through giant cottonwood trees with bright green leaves arcing toward the river.

Elijah immediately shimmied up a tree, Adeline peeled off her socks and shoes to wade in a pool of standing water, and Isaiah lobbed stone after stone into the murmuring river. Aayi sat in the shade, the shawl of her sari flapping in the breeze as she watched them play. Baba joined them all—removing his wet socks and sandals to dip his toes in the icy water, standing beneath the tree to watch Elijah, then selecting flat rocks to skip along the surface of the river next to Isaiah. I sat hugging my knees, ready to grab Isaiah if he lost his balance or ventured too far into the water.

"Do you swim here?" Baba asked me.

"I'm sure we could if we wanted to, but maybe it would be better when the water is not so high—or so cold," I said.

"We live near the largest river in India," he said, "so we all grew up learning to swim there." I imagined the river full of Indian children laughing, splashing, and throwing one another in the rushing water. Elijah had completed structured swimming lessons at the local indoor swimming pool, and he still couldn't swim.

Inviting Aayi and Baba here to "our" spot felt natural and good. And it had only taken us asking, then making room in the minivan for them to join us. Simple as it was, this felt like hospitality. We made space.

* * *

Hospitality doesn't have to be fancy, structured, or dramatic. Jay Pathak calls hospitality the "art of neighboring."[5] Rosaria Butterfield calls it "radically ordinary hospitality."[6] D. L. Mayfield calls it the "ministry of making Funfetti cake" (de-

livering cakes made from a box mix to neighbors).[7] Shannan
Martin, author of *The Ministry of Ordinary Places*, says she
and her husband have the "ministry of meetings."[8] And Kelley
Nikondeha calls it "durable hospitality."[9] Ascribing dignity to
another human being can be as simple as giving the neighbor
kids stale potato chips in the backyard while they run through
the sprinkler. Contact with other humans is the goal; connection is the calling.

Hospitality can be organized or organic, structured or
spontaneous, controlled or chaotic. It can include an intimate
dessert, a late-night board game, or a themed party. It can be
a monthly supper club with two other couples where we get
childcare and have adult conversation, a different couple taking turns cooking each time. It can be inviting neighbors over
via social media to sign up to play a game like Bunco once a
month. My aunt does this, and one of twelve participants hosts
each month, providing the appetizers.

Hospitality can include absorbing one or two children
into our three-ring-circus life to give another parent a break.
It can be welcoming foster children into our home, signing
up to be a Safe Family, or partnering with a recently arrived
refugee family to help them buy paper towels and school sup-
plies.[10] It can look like trick-or-treating with neighbor families
at Halloween, hosting an Easter egg hunt, or having a front
yard cookout on the Fourth of July. My friend Annie, who
is a Christian, celebrates Shabbat with her Jewish neighbors,
lighting candles, saying prayers, and joining in their ritual of
Sabbath. They have become the best of friends over the years,
though their beliefs differ.

Sometimes hospitality means being a joiner—attending
community events like book clubs at the local bookstore,

volunteering at a homeless shelter or 10K road race, or sitting in public meetings to tap into the pulse of the community. Although Adam and I enjoy leading, this stage of our life has hindered us from taking on additional responsibilities. So we've become all-star joiners. As an actor, Adam has found that performing in the local theater is a way to immerse himself in the community. I've visited the local Chinese center at the university to practice my Chinese and am exploring writer groups to meet other writers. Intentionally visiting different parks, libraries, and areas of town is another way I'm learning to dig deeper into the soil of my city and getting to know people outside my natural social circles.

Our generous God takes the minuscule seeds of the time, energy, or even desire we have to be hospitable and multiplies the fruit of our faith. Holy, humble, and community-building hospitality flourishes as we pursue relationships with people we know, and love the strangers we meet along the way.

*A small house will hold
a hundred friends.*

—**Kenyan proverb**

SEVEN

Beyond Our Limits

A woman with a million-dollar home hosted the kickoff for the women's ministry at Colorado Church Number Twelve. I held a lemon cupcake in one hand and raspberry-infused water in the other as my friend Liz and I admired the stunning view of the Rocky Mountains. I asked about her work with law enforcement and public schools in the city, educating them on sex trafficking prevention. She asked me about our kids and the search for a renter for our spare room.

"Would you be willing to have a formerly sex-trafficked girl coming out of jail live with you?" she asked.

I paused before answering. My thoughts collided and tripped over one another. "Possibly . . . ?" I trailed off. "I mean, maybe that's why we haven't found an international student yet. Maybe God had this in mind." I waited a second more, considering how to word my next questions: But do you think it'd be a good idea with three small children at home? Would it be safe?

The Western god is primarily concerned with safe journeys, smooth transitions, and a peaceful night's slumber—apparently. But the Jesus I read about in the Bible isn't so much worried about safety or comfort as concerned with slaying self, loving the unlovely, and giving until we gasp. When it came to safety, Jesus had some radical ideas about the terms of service for being a member of God's kingdom.

The lion Aslan presides over C. S. Lewis's mythical Narnia. In the series, a wooden wardrobe is a portal to a magical land where beavers talk and ordinary little boys and girls become kings and queens.

"Is he—quite safe?" Susan asks Mr. Beaver when she learns about the lion.

"Safe?" replies Mr. Beaver. "Who said anything about safe? 'Course he isn't safe. But he's good. He's the King, I tell you."[1]

When we fall in love with Jesus, what are the stakes, exactly? How do we live for a good God who isn't necessarily predictable or safe? Often, we must leap the first hurdle to Spirit-led hospitality: a concern for our own comfort, security, and safety.

"You know," I answered Liz, "we might be open to having someone live with us."

What would have happened if, during key periods of history, the helpers hadn't been willing to take a risk? How would choosing security and comfort over change have impacted the effectiveness of the Underground Railroad, the transformation of laws and policies brought about by the civil rights movement, or the rescuing of refugees fleeing Iraq and Syria? Our silence can signify complicity, and our fear can lead us to take cover rather than engage.

Some Christians during the Holocaust admitted that they tried to distance themselves because they felt powerless to do anything. Sometimes I wonder, horrified, if I would have done the same thing. One Christian man, who lived in Germany during World War II, shared his haunting story:

> A railroad track ran behind our small church, and each Sunday morning we could hear the whistle in the distance and then the wheels coming over the tracks. We became disturbed when we heard the cries coming from the train as it passed by. We realized that it was carrying Jews like cattle in the cars!
>
> Week after week the whistle would blow. We dreaded to hear the sound of those wheels because we knew that we would hear the cries of the Jews en route to a death camp. Their screams tormented us.
>
> We knew the time the train was coming, and when we heard the whistle blow we began singing hymns. By the time the train came past our church, we were singing at the top of our voices. If we heard the screams, we sang more loudly and soon we heard them no more.
>
> Years have passed, and no one talks about it anymore. But I still hear that train whistle in my sleep. God forgive me; forgive all of us who called ourselves Christians yet did nothing to intervene.[2]

Although Europe was majority Christian at the time of the Holocaust, less than 1 percent of Christians actively helped the Jews.[3] The Dutch Christian Corrie ten Boom, who hid Jews during the Holocaust, once carried a Jewish infant downstairs in her home to show her pastor. Instead of praising her for protecting the baby, he scolded her for breaking the law and sheltering Jews. Her father was in the room with them and interjected, "You say we could lose our lives for this child.

I would consider that the greatest honor that could come to my family."[4]

Perhaps the Spirit will not lead us into harrowing circumstances to serve God. But God still whispers for us to seek one stranger—perhaps a person already on our Jericho road—to stand by, support, and speak out for. What would happen if every Christ-follower helped one person in need? One person coming out of sex trafficking, one struggling teenager, one lonely international student, one foster child, one person who is homeless, one jail inmate, one person addicted to drugs, one single mother? How would helping just one person transform our families, jails, streets, churches, public schools, and hospitals? Instead, we outsource hospitality, and the church misses out on the wisdom of those who have suffered.

* * *

I felt conflicted about having a sex-trafficked young woman live with us. I wondered how it would challenge and stretch Adam and me as a couple. As Elijah picked the story before bed, I thought about how it might affect the kids. Handing me the randomly selected library book, he and Adeline cuddled up next to me as I began reading. In the book, a little boy named William drinks cocoa, fluffs his pillow, and snuggles into bed. But he is awakened by a tapping sound—a chipmunk at his window begs to come inside. Three other woodland creatures do the same until they have a full bed.

Then a note slides under the door. "Do you have room for just one more?" an unknown animal has written.

They confer and decide not to welcome anyone else—unless the animal is small enough to fit in bed. William opens the door and finds a giant bear standing outside. They refuse to let him in, but immediately regret their decision and beckon the bear back, shouting, "Wait! We'll scooch a bit. There's room for six—somehow we'll fit."[5]

The final illustration of the book shows five animals in bed and William sleeping cozily on a rocking chair. I wiped my eyes as I closed the book, surprised that we had happened to pick a picture book about hospitality.

"Is it a happy cry?" Adeline asked, noticing my tears.

"Yes, yes it is," I said. Sort of. Honestly, I mostly winced in the bright light cast on my truest self. Was I putting a placeholder in my life for God to insert love for a stranger? Was I generous with my time, possessions, and emotions? Did I have space for one more? Was I willing to sleep on the hard rocking chair to make space for the person in need at an inconvenient time? Most of the time, I had to admit, my answer was no.

* * *

With small children at home, my branches feel stripped and bare, pruned to the nub. Spiritual and personal growth seem dormant and invisible. Adam and I have come to refer to this season as The Narrowing. I'm surviving, not thriving, hunkering down and conserving energy until this season passes. Beautiful and brutal, sacred and oh-so-ordinary, this stage of life has been my most challenging by far. But even in my scarcity, Jesus is gloriously, annoyingly unrelenting. He's still asking me to give.

Adam and I were still in discussions about opening our home to the young woman, exploring the possibilities. One morning, I read the Bible on the back porch while Adam fed the kids breakfast. I had awoken three times in the night to tend to children; the first one was up at four o'clock and refused to go back to sleep. The new day promised little more than the predictability of wiping wee bottoms, taming tantrums, and making meals. Leaning back in my chair, I observed the signs of life all around me and breathed the autumn air.

An artisan spider rewove her glistening web on the porch railing just as she did day after day. As I watched, I felt that we were kindred spirits, bound by our similarly Sisyphean tasks. I sympathized with her fortitude and hoped for an ounce of her dedication. I wondered whether she also started her day with a sigh, thinking, Didn't I do this already?

That morning, I just happened to be reading about this type of exhaustion. The disciples understood bone-tired weariness. They traveled in pairs and stayed at strangers' houses by night, healing and teaching about Christ by day. When they reported back to Jesus, he promised them a quiet retreat with him. Instead, they ended up in a crowd of thousands of hungry people. And Jesus took them past their limits, saying, "*You* give them something to eat" (Luke 9:13, my emphasis).

I reflected on that for a minute, continuing to watch my spider friend. I could relate on a small scale to being forced to feed people utterly dependent on me for their next meal. The disciples must have looked at Jesus as if he had two heads. I expect they felt physically, emotionally, and spiritually drained. Had Jesus dared ask even *more* of them? Hadn't they spent every second over the last weeks vaulting selfishness to serve him? They didn't even have their own food to offer, but they scrambled to find a few loaves and fish from a young boy.

The Saturday after studying this passage, I met a couple who was homeless on the sidewalk holding a cardboard sign and an eight-month-old baby. I wore my own clean, clothed, well-fed infant on my chest, and I imagined what it would be like to stand on the street begging for his next meal. I handed the couple some cash within minutes of beginning to chat with them. But that was the easy part. I felt compelled to get their phone number, and they came to mind several times through-out the week. But like the disciples, I found myself thinking, Jesus, what can I do? I have my own family to feed and care for. And did I mention that I'm exhausted? Are you daring to ask even more of me?

You give them something to eat, God seemed to say as I journaled about the situation one morning soon after meeting the family. Later that day, I texted them to see if they could meet up for lunch at a deli the next week. I had no idea what to do after that, but I trusted that the timing of meditating on the feeding of the five thousand was no coincidence.

My two-year relationship with that family didn't turn into the mutual friendship that I had hoped for. But I learned that Jesus exceeds the time, monetary, and physical limits we set for ourselves to take us beyond our thresholds. And what do we find there? What do we find when we blow past our lim-its? I wish I could say I immediately found a bedrock of grace, strength, and love. I wish I could say that I always found kind words and compassion. But often what I find when I exceed my own limits in order to follow God's way is a new awareness of how selfish and prideful I am. Sometimes I let weariness win as I complain that, like the spider, I'll have to reweave the web all over again tomorrow. But somehow God makes a strong web out of my stilted efforts. And then the Spirit enables me to do it all over again.

* * *

Before we moved from our rental house to the home we bought several miles away, I told our Saudi friend Norah that I planned for the kids to share a room so we could have a guest room. "What do you do for guests when they stay with you in Saudi Arabia?" I asked, curious.

"We usually give up our own rooms to offer them the best room in the house," she answered.

The gospel of Mark tells the story of Jesus watching the widow who crept up to offer her two copper coins to the treasury in the temple (Mark 12:41-44). Although outwardly it was a meager offering, Jesus pointed out that she put in more than all the others. The others gave out of the surplus of their wealth, but she gave out of her poverty. She offered all she had to live on. How would this influence our love of God and others if we gave out of our poverty instead of out of our excess?

The Giving Tree by Shel Silverstein is a story about a tree that loves a boy throughout his life. The tree offers him apples to sell, branches to build a home, and its trunk to build a boat, until it has nothing left to give. In the final scene, the tree gives the boy, now elderly, its stump to sit on and rest. "And the tree was happy," the book ends.[6] I'm not sure if I like the book, actually. The boy comes across as selfish, only taking from the tree; the tree seems to be in an unhealthy, codependent relationship. Yet perhaps this is a picture of Christlike, sacrificial love and all the little deaths to self that fertilize the soil of relationships. Jesus gives without expecting anything in return.

Elijah is one of my favorite characters in the Bible, so much so that I named my first son after him. Elijah is often homeless, and frequently on the run. In 1 Kings 17, he is physically and emotionally depleted, so God orders the ravens to care for him. Soon after that he takes refuge in the home of a woman, called the widow of Zarephath, whom God also commanded to help Elijah. While I sometimes identify with the bone-weary Elijah, sometimes I see myself in the ravens and the widow—those who are planted in a place, have resources to share, and are willing to listen to the voice of God commanding them to provide for those in need. Perhaps God is asking us to offer our leaves, branches, or trunk in the form of our space, time, attention, or listening ear? Perhaps providing for the needs of others is less about Bible knowledge and more about sitting with someone and giving whatever small offering we happen to have right then.

I once read about calling a guest room the "Christ room."[7] What if we designated one room in our house as a "Christ room"? Or if we don't have such a room, what if we reserved one chair at our table or one seat in our car that we invite someone else to fill? What if we reserved one night in our schedules to ask someone to join our home or life? Do I have room to spare? Could I scooch over a bit to make room for Christ?

* * *

We were still not sure about opening our home to the nineteen-year-old woman coming out of jail. I spoke with a person who worked at the jail and with another woman who ran a non-profit helping women coming out of prostitution.

"But do you think this is a good idea?" I kept asking, hoping that someone would tell us no. "I mean, we have tiny children. Would it be wise to have someone coming out of jail live with us? Would it be *safe*?" They couldn't say. It was our choice.

We wondered about the wisdom of having a woman who had experienced abuse live with us when Adam worked from home. How would she—and he—feel if they were alone together making turkey sandwiches in the kitchen? Would she invite her old friends around? Would those friends put our children in danger? There were so many unknowns.

I called my mother-in-law. A former labor and delivery nurse, she's one of the most compassionate women I know. She had helped many formerly incarcerated women, and I hoped for some guidance from her. She shared about the various women she had known over the years, and admitted that she had been taken advantage of and felt that at times the contact had exposed her two youngest sons to more than they were ready for.

"But would you do it again? Knowing what you know now, would you do it again?" I asked, clutching the phone and hiding in the kitchen as the kids played loudly in the other room.

Without pausing, thinking, or qualifying, she answered, "In a heartbeat."

Living for Jesus is not logical. You can make a pro/con chart about decisions that extend hospitality or sacrifice comfort. But the sides will never be equally weighted, because the Spirit, faith, and the mystery of God cannot be quantified. We hadn't yet officially said we would welcome the young woman, but we kept asking questions, researching, praying, listening, and taking the next step.

I admit that fear found a footing, clawing its way up my body and holding my eyelids open at night. Would I somehow be putting my own children in harm's way? But I also knew from experience that fear is not always a valid reason to *not* do something. If it were, I never would have knowingly taught in a failing school in Chicago, I never would have quit my job and relocated to Communist China or lived in Uganda or Tajikistan, I never would have risked falling in love with an actor ten thousand miles away, and I never would have attempted to have children. Sometimes fear is a signal to fight or flee, but often fear is faith's phantom.

I scribbled in my journal at dawn one day, "God, I have never wanted the American Dream. Poke holes in it to make room for your Spirit. I would rather be uncomfortable, inconvenienced, and scraping by and know I am smack in the center of something way bigger than me, than living for myself."

Sometimes we and our children must follow God into dangerous circumstances. And sometimes dangerous circumstances just seem dangerous because they're unfamiliar. When I'm not sure whether faith or fear has me in its grip, I move through the next open door. And then I move through the next one after that, praying, asking, begging all the way: Jesus, if this isn't your plan, slam the door shut. Paul did much the same, going with his gut until the Spirit barred him from entering Asia (Acts 16:6-7). We step and pray, wait and watch; step and pray, wait and watch.

The door slammed shut. Before we had decided whether to move forward, the young woman left jail and promptly disappeared. Honestly? Relief flooded me, because we didn't have to do the Hard Thing after all.

God does not force us to move, join, initiate, or invite, but waits on the sidelines until we're ready and open to God's irrational, wild, and unpredictable love. The mantra "Do not fear" flows through the Bible like a tincture to soothe God's trembling followers. Encountering God led to quaking knees and wet knickers, but fear as a signal of God's way was usually a farce.

Ananias had every reason to be petrified of Paul. As a Pharisee, Paul (then called Saul) had sought out, tortured, and slaughtered followers of Jesus. So when Saul had a change of heart and announced his conversion, the Christians weren't quick to welcome him into the fold. One day as a certain disciple named Ananias was praying, God spoke his name, "Ananias." Ananias's answer?

"Here I am, Lord," he said (Acts 9:10 NRSV).

God instructed him to find a man named Saul. At first, Ananias argued with God, saying—my paraphrase—"But Lord, I've heard about this guy and how he hurt your people." God told him to go despite his hesitations. And so he went. He put his hands on Saul and called him brother. He prayed for restored sight and Holy Spirit fuel. Spiny scales fell from Saul's eyes, and he rose, got baptized, ate, and gathered strength. Then God used him to transform history.

What if fear had so crippled Ananias that he didn't go find the terrorist, Saul? Perhaps God would have raised up someone else. Yet Ananias would have forfeited the experience of witnessing God rip off the scales, inflate Paul with Spirit power, and accelerate him into the ministry of reconciliation in the world.

This wild, unscripted journey began with Ananias being available to God's voice. He listened, heard, then answered, "Here I am, Lord." Perhaps God desires for us to also listen for the Spirit's voice and consider the strangers, friends, and neighbors in our path, extending shaky hands as we pray, "Here I am, Lord."

If you can't live longer,
live deeper.

—**Italian proverb**

EIGHT

Solitude

One spring afternoon in China, I sipped chrysanthemum tea with Hannah, my Chinese friend who had urged me to pray for the right-next-to-you people. The refrigerator in the living room hummed, and construction vehicles screeched in the vacant lot behind my apartment. During my second year of language school for Mandarin Chinese—and my fifth year in China—my Christian organization had advised that I study spiritual content I wouldn't learn from my secular Chinese teachers. Hannah agreed to teach me words like *gospel*, *grace*, *heaven*, *salvation*, and *Holy Spirit* in Chinese. Our conversation veered off course as we began to discuss the differences between Chinese and Western cultures, particularly when it came to followers of Jesus she knew from northwest and northeast China compared to the Christians she had known from the United States.

"We've learned so much from our Western Christian friends," she said, holding a small, handleless teacup decorated with bluebirds and coral peonies.

I was skeptical. What could a passionate Chinese Christian learn from a structured and busy Westerner? I had started to favor Eastern culture over Western culture, enamored by my Chinese friends' elevation of the group over the individual. Living in another culture had made me hyperaware of my own cultural flaws.

She continued, "One problem I see with Chinese Christians is that our discipleship is usually done in groups instead of in pairs like it is in the West." I gazed through the smudged window to where I could hear the staccato of someone chopping vegetables across the courtyard. Although meeting with a group to know Jesus, study the Bible, and learn together sounded fine to me, I could see the downsides of not having someone know me personally. I might form an unhealthy codependency on the group to meet with God, not recognizing I could remove my sandals at any time and find myself standing on holy ground.

Although most American churches have a long way to go when it comes to authentic community and intentional hospitality, one strength of the Western church is the belief that we were created as individuals. Most Western churches highlight that we are known, cherished, and adored by a Creator who desires intimacy with us. Since I was a teenager, I've memorized verses about God rejoicing over me with singing, counting every strand of hair on my head, and knitting the threads of my body, soul, and spirit together in my mother's womb. In the Western church, though sometimes to a fault, we relish our identity as unique sons or daughters of the King, forgiven and loved because of Jesus.

"Western Christians also have this idea of private space and time that's kind of unknown to Chinese," Hannah said. I knew what she meant. My Chinese students found it peculiar that I shopped, traveled, exercised, and wandered the city alone. To them, it wasn't normal to engage in solitary activities.

"But I think it's good that you guys do that," she said. She then told me a story. "One day a Western friend of mine told my husband and me that he was too busy to hang out with us. Later in the day, I happened to be passing his house and knocked on his door. I was surprised to find him there doing nothing. 'I thought you said you were busy?' I said. He answered that he *was* busy—being alone. 'Six days of the week I see people, so this is exactly what I need to be doing right now,' he said. I was shocked, but my husband, Sam, and I adopted this new idea and now set aside time for solitude too."

Although individualism and privacy can be problematic, individualism can help us believe that we are beloved children of God, uniquely and personally known. Privacy permits us to carve out time for contemplation, solitude, and Sabbath— necessary ingredients for renewal and spiritual replenishment possibly not as easily enjoyed by people from more collectivist cultures.

As the shadows shifted in the room, Hannah asked, "Do you want to try praying in Chinese?" I fumbled through a prayer in Mandarin, feeling a bit more fluent than the previous week even though I used the word *dictionary* instead of *grace*. As Hannah prayed next, I listened to the richness of her inner life with Jesus, spoken aloud for me to witness. Her prayer was a sweet conversation with her Savior and loving friend.

* * *

Sometimes I feel frustrated by contemplatives like Thomas Merton and Henri Nouwen. I wonder if they had any idea what it is like to be a parent or work at a stressful job. For those of us who are not priests, nuns, or monks, solitude seems like a luxury, not a necessity. Despite a reticence toward solitary activities, people in the area of northwest China where I lived still took a *xiu xi*, or rest time, each day. Adults and children all went home from work and school to eat lunch together, then napped until around two o'clock, when they resumed their jobs and classes. Rest was a necessity, not a reward—a right, not a privilege. From the wealthy men and women working in government offices to the butcher with a cot on the bloodstained concrete below a fly-covered carcass, nap time was a must. My Chinese friends explained that at noon, our energy reserves were lowest, because this was when the yang was switching over to the yin. The sun was swapping out light for darkness, so naturally our energy was at its lowest. They felt sorry for me if I missed my nap, and eventually I felt sorry for me too.

Before living in China, I'd always felt bad about napping. Some of my earliest memories of my father are of him yanking the covers off my feet no later than nine o'clock and boasting about all he had accomplished while I lazed about in bed. Many of us in the West one-up one another about who is the most tired.

Productivity is usually increased by rest, not competitive exhaustion. But as followers of Jesus, we don't just seek solitude and rest to increase our productivity (although this is a fringe benefit). Sleep satiates our souls, not just our bodies. Solitude roots us firmly in the love of God so we can love others: "We love because [God] first loved us" (1 John 4:19). We can't siphon love out of empty vessels. Solitude replenishes us so that we can practice hospitality, flourish in our communities, and love our neighbors.

Fortunately, God devised a rhythm of rest for us. Sabbath enables us to keep opening our lives to love God and others. God lists Sabbath among the Ten Commandments the children of God were to honor first (Exodus 20:8). Sabbath was not an option, but an obligation for God's people—a boundary of rest intended to benefit not just our souls but our communities as well. Jesus knew there was intrinsic value in sleep, prayer, and solitude. Jesus constantly snuck away to be alone—even purposely to places called "lonely" (Luke 5:16).

* * *

I arrived at the Abbey of St. Walburga just north of Fort Collins one spring morning. As a birthday gift, Adam had surprised me with a one-night retreat at this secluded Benedictine monastery for nuns and retreat-goers, just fifty minutes from our house near the Colorado-Wyoming border. Sister Elizabeth, a tall, thin nun in her fifties wearing a cheery apron over her black habit, showed me to my private room overlooking the abbey's small cattle farm. She informed me that hot meals would be provided in the cafeteria, and I was welcome to attend the seven prayer times if I liked.

Giddy over the silence but nervous I might squander the time, I noted I had about an hour before the first prayer time. After putting on sunscreen, I pocketed note cards, my key, and my phone, then sauntered down the road toward the bench I had noticed on my drive in. What should I think about? How should I pray? Who should I pray for?

Just enjoy the silence, I told myself. Try listening.

After strolling down the road, I forced myself to sit on a bench and be still. A small stream lullabied through fields of lush pasture. So this is what quiet feels like, I thought. Birds chirped, grasshoppers clicked, bees buzzed, cows lowed, frogs called, invisible birds rustled in bushes, and the wind whispered to spring's blushing trees.

I started to pray, then stopped myself. I got off the bench, squatted down, and inspected a large rock to the left of my feet. The rock was speckled with orange, white, black, and glinting silver. I leaned in, willing myself to notice detail. Light green, soft gray, and rusty orange lichen lay like bumpy star stickers on the surface of the rock. I peered again. This time, I noticed nearly microscopic black bugs darting around on the lichen. A black ant striding by must have looked hulkish to them. I remembered a poem I had read recently, comparing the Holy Spirit to geckos, chameleons, and iguanas.[1] Maybe the Holy Spirit is like these black dot bugs, I thought—only evident to those who take the time to notice them and celebrate their existence in the world. This seemed like evidence that creation is not just for people, that God hides some beauty in secret places—such as brilliant sea creatures in the icy ocean depths—where only God can see and delight.

Sitting back down on the bench, I squeezed my knees to my chest. Sunshine soaked into the skin on my arms, neck, face, and the tops of my sandaled feet. I knew my freckles would multiply themselves by the time I got home, but it was worth it. This—this nature, sunshine, and quiet—fed my soul, refilling my empty well. Lately, life had been much like Colorado reservoirs in the summertime—emptied, but never refilled. I relied on my past times of solitude to fill my present lack, but my levels were alarmingly low.

I decided to return in time for sext, the midday prayer. Carefully picking my way through the tall blades of grass to avoid the dried cow patties, I scanned the field for rattlesnakes. I took too many pictures on the way back but wanted to document my first personal retreat—the first time I had gotten away alone since I had returned from China eight years before to get married.

I slipped quietly into the chapel. Since I'm not Catholic, I wasn't sure if I should make the sign of the cross, kneel, or make some other holy motion before sitting. I counted twenty-three nuns sitting in rows facing one another at the front of the chapel. I hushed my inner soundtrack that automatically began humming songs from *The Sound of Music*. I unfolded the order of service I had grabbed from the back of the chapel to read and sing along.

A bell rang and the nuns stood, regal in their formal habits, robes rustling like leaves. Their ages seemed to span from young twenties to elderly women in wheelchairs. Some wore ivory veils, but most wore black, their modesty reminding me of my devoted Muslim friends in hijabs and abayas, who also prayed at set times each day. One woman sang out, then all the other voices joined in unison, the shock of twenty-three a capella female voices a stunning change when I was used to mixed-gender, untrained voices. The notes of Gregorian chant bounced around the high ceilings of the chapel. I tried to follow along with words printed in the order of service as the nuns sang, but the repetitive chanting—like a rowboat rocking back and forth, back and forth—lulled my thoughts away from the page.

My Protestant brain had questions. I wondered if many Catholics had such adoration for Mary because she was the closest person they had to a female image of the divine. I wanted to know if these nuns laughed hysterically like the nuns in the movies I'd seen, or if they had petty fights among one another when they had PMS. (I had seen a giant delivery of sanitary pads near the front door.) Did they always feel close to God? Did they sometimes wish they had husbands to warm their cold feet at night or children to snuggle under their arms? Did they ever regret their decision to cloister themselves from the rest of the world? Did they understand pain and suffering, poverty and injustice? Did they drink beer?

As usual, my thoughts distracted me from opportunities to delve beyond the surface into the deeps. But following the physical cues of sitting, standing, kneeling, and making the sign of the cross by drawing my fingers from forehead to chest, left shoulder to right shoulder, brought me back to the moment. Holy water flung in my face, candles flickering, incense wafting down the aisle, and physically moving my hands to make the sign of the cross or to pound my chest in confession: all these gestures felt full of significance. Going through the motions can often drag our stubborn hearts along for the ride.

Benedictine monks and nuns follow the spiritual scaffolding of the liturgy of the hours, sometimes called the divine hours. When they weren't milking cows, making cheese, or tending bees, the nuns at this particular abbey attended seven different prayer times a day. They sang through the entire book of Psalms in a week. My only other experience with the liturgy of the hours was when Isaiah was a newborn. I downloaded an app on my phone called the Divine Hours that offered the liturgy of prayers, hymns, and Scriptures to read. It turned out that the many nursing times a day often lined up perfectly with the rhythm of the liturgy. With a baby and two other little people to care for, this was often the only spiritual nourishment I received.

Carving out time for solitude is especially challenging in certain seasons of life. I love the story of Susanna, the mom of John and Charles Wesley, praying in the kid chaos with her apron slung over her head.[2] In the Old Testament, the tabernacle was the portable dwelling place of the Spirit of God throughout the Israelites' wanderings in the wilderness. Sometimes all we can manage are prayers haphazardly flung to God from the center of our kitchens, cars, or cubicles-turned-tabernacles.

Sometimes, like the tabernacle, spirituality has to be portable. My friend with ten children leaves a Bible open in every room, just in case she has a minute to take a glance. While we're driving to work or even heating oatmeal in the microwave, we can listen to spiritual music or podcasts that lead us to meditate on certain Scripture passages. We can follow Bible reading plans using an app on our phones or read a short devotional book. The goal of these scraps of solitude in our frantic days is intimacy with Jesus. Solitude—even for five minutes a day—reminds us that God is with us and leading us to love others in the world. Solitude centers us in the cistern of God's love.

As we forsake frenzy to find our rootedness in God, we'll have the strength to support the people God brings into our life. Jesus says, "If you make yourselves at home with me and my words are at home in you, you can be sure that whatever you ask will be listened to and acted upon" (John 15:7 *The Message*). When we make ourselves at home in the love of God, we can find the security we need to be able to serve others.

I glanced around the chapel and noticed the multiple triangular windows wedged between the ponderosa pine walls.

Light could enter in every season, at every time of day. I marveled at the metaphor of God finding a different angle into every season of our lives as well. The nuns rose to exit, proceeding down the aisle in pairs, and I caught a glimpse of their footwear, all sturdy and expensive brands. Even saints need sensible footwear to traipse their holy roads.

* * *

I sometimes wonder if God has different expectations for introverts and extroverts when it comes to hospitality. When do personality profiles, labels, and tests like the Enneagram and Myers-Briggs become a crutch? When are they a life-giving practice, leading us to become healthier, fuller, more neighborly people?

My husband, Adam, reminds me of Frog in the Frog and Toad stories our Iranian friend, Rahim, loves so much. Our kids know the exact story that is representative of their daddy. The story, "Alone," begins with Toad reading a note from his best friend, Frog, who says he'll be out for the day, but that he wants to be alone. Toad, in true extrovert fashion, doesn't get it. Toad spots his introverted friend sitting on an island by himself and says to himself, "Poor Frog, he must be very sad. I will cheer him up." He runs home to prepare food to bring to Frog. Toad convinces a turtle to carry him to Frog, and Toad begins thinking Frog doesn't want to be his friend anymore. As soon as Toad arrives on the island, he blurts out an apology for all the dumb things he's done. Frog says that just because he wanted to be alone doesn't mean he doesn't care about Toad. He just wanted to be alone to think about his wonderful life.[3]

If it were up to my introverted husband, he would be alone 80 percent of the time. He recharges through solitary activities, while I absorb energy from people as fast as an appliance drains power from an electrical socket. After parties, we face one another in bed, knees and noses nearly touching. I rehash the evening in great detail, while his eyelids involuntarily slide shut for the night.

Perhaps introverts and extroverts are the yin and yang of community: trading strengths and weaknesses in the ebb and flow of energy. Introverts rely on extroverts to ask questions and put their own self-consciousness on the shelf to initiate and carry conversations. Extroverts depend on introverts to balance them out, keeping them dancing just enough, but not so much that they spin out of control and become too dizzy to dance.

Every roommate I had over the past twenty years was an introvert. My first-year roommate in college initially puzzled me. How could she just laze about on her bed for hours at a time when there were so many amazing things she could be doing? After college, both my roommates in Chicago were introverted. They taught me that relaxing and reading, or sitting and doing nothing at all, could still fall under the umbrella of the abundant life.

Introverts keep extroverts balanced and healthy. Adam helps me set limits, and I sometimes push him beyond his, but neither of us is more holy than the other. The danger is when we put personality test labels before devotion to God or a commitment to love our neighbors as we love ourselves. And unfortunately as humans, our default devotion is usually love of self, not love of others.

Although Adam helps me with boundaries and burnout, he still values relationships. As we go over the calendar and make scheduling decisions, he often says, "When in doubt, choose community." I once prayed about whether to keep supporting a friend in full-time ministry when I myself was about to begin raising support to go to China. I felt that God told me something that has become a mantra: "Err on the side of generosity." I want to err on the side of love, generosity, having an open home, and inviting people even when I don't always feel like it. Then again, we also need systems of solitude and rhythms of rest, renewal, and recharging. We can't pour into people out of an empty well. Our reservoirs must have a sustainable Source.

One early morning, long before the sun rose, Jesus got up, left the house, and disappeared to a solitary place to pray. Simon and some others looked for him, and when they found him they said, "Everyone is looking for you!" This story reminds me of my children, padding downstairs to find me before six o'clock. Unlike Jesus, I'm usually annoyed that my alone time has been interrupted before I even finish a single cup of coffee. But Jesus responded, "Let us go somewhere else—to the nearby villages—so I can preach there also. That is why I have come" (Mark 1:35-38). Jesus walked the tension rope between solitude and service.

Jesus never told people not to bother him or acted resentful. He was willing to stop, listen, touch, and pay attention to the people who approached him. The time he spent alone with God fueled the time he spent with people, but he also knew that hiding away wouldn't fulfill his mission to embody the kingdom on earth. Jesus' every sense was tenderized by the Spirit.

But what kinds of boundaries *should* we have to avoid hospitality fatigue and burnout? Should we welcome *anyone* who wants to come to our homes? Should we have people over every night of the week? When should we say no to a request for help, or to an invitation to someone's home?

Although we can use boundaries as excuses not to love the difficult people in our lives, it's comforting to know that even Jesus had social limits. When Jesus withdrew with the disciples to a lake, a large crowd followed. Instead of turning them away, "he told his disciples to have a small boat ready for him, to keep the people from crowding him" (Mark 3:7-10). The people knew they could be healed by touching Jesus, so the crowds pressed in, threatening to crush him. He didn't abandon the masses of people who needed him; he stepped into a boat, then drifted a short distance from the shore to continue preaching. The floating boat was a boundary.

Even activists like Dorothy Day had boundaries. She wrote, "You must know when to find your own, quiet moment of solitude. But you must know when to open the door to go be with others, and you must know *how* to open the door. There's no point in opening the door with bitterness and resentment in your heart." Day recounted a memory of a time she internalized the importance of setting boundaries: "I remember one day realizing that the best, the very best, I could do for everyone in the community, including our guests, was to stay away, to not fight staying away, which I might have done successfully. There are times when one's generosity is a mask for one's pride: what will 'they' do without me?"[4] Is it possible that we may think we are serving others, when in fact we are striving to serve ourselves?

When our acts of service turn to badges of honor, it's time to take a break. When we resent our guests or feel drained rather than filled after we host, it's time to reassess the source of our service. And when duty takes the place of devotion to

God and others, then we may need to escape the crowds and sit in silence.

Most of us don't err on the side of radical generosity. In my experience, I need fewer boundaries and more courage. Cultivating our inner life can calibrate us to God's plans. When we reserve space for prayer, listening, Bible reading, communal worship, and connecting with God in Sabbath, solitude, and creativity, God gives us wisdom about which activities to cut and which ones to keep. Listening and love help us gauge the fine line between selfishness and self-care.

* * *

During dinner at the abbey I sat with two women who knew one another. I had spent eight hours in solitude and I was eager to hear human voices again. They had driven up from Denver and were from the same oblate, they said. I nodded, having no idea what an oblate was, though I assumed it meant they went to the same church. As we finished eating, one woman asked me how old my kids were.

"One, three, and five," I said, scooping up a bite of mashed potatoes onto my fork. "It's a lot," I added after seeing their expressions.

"Enjoy your time with them," one of the women cautioned me. "It goes so fast. And once it's gone, it's gone and you don't get it back."

Her response reminded me of something by Henri Nouwen that I had read earlier in the day. I was surprised that as someone without children, he had the gall to write about parenthood. But perhaps his undistracted viewpoint elevated his objective wisdom. His words pierced me. Nouwen wrote, "Children are not properties to own and rule over, but gifts to cherish. Our children are our most important guests, who enter into our home, ask for careful attention, stay for a while and then leave to follow their own way. Children are strangers whom we have to get to know."[5]

Sometimes in the middle of the shrieking, whining, and intensity of parenting, I look at Adam and whisper, "You, I *chose*. But *them* . . ." Yet in all the frustration and exhaustion, I know my children are strangers strategically placed in my particular family. Our children live with us temporarily until they find their home in the world. Do I show *them* the same respect and hospitality I show nonfamily members?

Family is our first tier of hospitality. We share our gifts, our presence, and our struggles only for a time. If we can't love, serve, or honor our families, how can we expect to love our friends, neighbors, and the ones we tend to loathe rather than love?

Solitude opened the door for deeper, more intentional community—beginning with the souls sitting around my crumb-crusted kitchen table every day. Solitude increased my gratitude for the people in my life.

Thomas Merton wrote, "We do not go into the desert to escape people but to learn how to find them."[6] There is a direct correlation between the energy we're able to conserve from times in solitude and our capacity for invitation. As I drove away from the abbey later that day, I felt ready to face my people. The nuns had played host to me, a stranger, offering me living water and heavenly bread. The inner rooms of my soul were swept clean and ready for guests once again.

A single stick may smoke,
but it will not burn.

—Ethiopian proverb

NINE

Utterly Dependent

The kids and I tucked cold toes under blankets on the couch and balanced popcorn bowls on our laps to watch a rendition of the Christmas story called *The Star*. I wondered how to detangle myth from fact as I discussed it with them afterward.

As an American, I grew up hearing (and telling) the Christmas story like this: Mary and Joseph travel alone to Bethlehem to register for the census. Mary goes into labor, and they desperately travel door-to-door searching for lodging. Rejected by the inn, Mary gives birth in a stable to an audience of nosy animals. They are visited by shepherds and eventually by wise men. Heaven and angels sing. The end.

But lately I've begun to discover how much I've superimposed Western culture on my reading of the Bible, filling in gaps with faulty assumptions. Keeping in mind the collectivist values of most non-Western cultures, doesn't it make sense to assume that Mary and Joseph embodied these values as well?

What if they weren't cast out, but shown greater hospitality than we could imagine?

In *Jesus through Middle Eastern Eyes*, scholar Kenneth Bailey shares a different Christmas story that takes into account most Middle Easterners' commitment to hospitality, group identity, and filial piety—that is, care for one's parents. In Bailey's retelling, the holy family of the lineage of David traveling to Bethlehem, the city of David, would not have been friendless. Far from the inept and unprepared husband that Joseph sometimes seems to be according to our Western reading, he likely would have prearranged for a place for his pregnant wife to stay during their time in Bethlehem. In the private two-room home that Bailey describes, they weren't able to stay in the guest room (translated "inn" in most English Bible translations), because that room was already occupied. Bailey suggests that the host welcomed Mary and Joseph into his or her very own room—a room shared with the animals at night.[1] Far from alone, Mary and Joseph would have been surrounded by midwives and birth attendants, neighbors and family members.

Rather than a bootstrapping, underdog story of isolation, independence, and individualism, the birth of Jesus was a tale of grand hospitality toward a tiny guest and his royal family. As it turns out, Emmanuel, God with us, blasted into humanity as the littlest beggar, utterly dependent on the hospitality of others.

* * *

My first year in China, Ma Li, a student from my college English class, nervously invited me to her home in the countryside for the weekend during winter break. I boarded the bus with my student and her friend and settled into a seat by the icy windowpane. The city buildings ended and we rolled through a vast sweep of land running up to dimpled mountains in the distance that looked like gray balloons about to burst. Poplar trees with naked branches pierced the ground like arrows. Crusty fields stretched out under a light dusting of snow, but in spring, congregations of sunflowers would worship heaven until the sun overwhelmed them and they'd bow their heads as summer waned.

Ma Li and her friend, Shu Wen Ping, crunched sunflower seeds, expertly deshelling them with their mouths and spitting the soft husks into a plastic bag. They chattered in the local dialect and occasionally asked me shaky questions, ashamed of their English but eager to practice just the same. I resigned myself to the discomfort of a myriad of unknowns.

"Get off here!" Ma Li announced as the bus sputtered to a stop three hours later. Ma Li linked her arm through mine as if I were an elderly woman in need of support, steering me around potholes and ruts in the road. I glanced around at the first of several hamlets we passed on our walk to Ma Li's home. A mini mosque with turquoise pagodas offered an artistic touch to the smooth mud homes of the village. Colorful, quilted blankets flapped over doors as barriers to the grit of spring dust storms and bitter winter winds. After a thirty-minute walk, we approached a metal gate and stepped into the courtyard of Ma Li's home.

Entering one of the three buildings within the courtyard, I scanned the single room. A brick floor stretched out under a coal stove, rickety table with stools, and large concrete bed called a *kang* that hugged the corner. From previous visits to the countryside, I knew that residents inserted a flame into an opening in the wall on the outside the house. This lit the manure inside the bed and warmed those sleeping on it through the chill of the night. I later learned that an outhouse hid in back, concealing a rectangular hole in the ground and a stack of newspaper used for toilet paper.

Ma Li's mother pressed her hand inside my shirt sleeves and pant legs, assessing the thickness of my long underwear. I passed the first test. But she said I should sit by the fire while everyone else prepared supper.

"Does she need to rest?" she asked her daughter.

I answered for myself in Chinese, "No, thanks. Can I help?"

"Oh, no, no. Just have a rest," she said, swirling oil in the giant wok heated by coal under the tiled kitchen counter. I rubbed my hands together by the cast iron stove until they tingled, watching the bustle and trying to be a good guest, though I felt awkward and out of place.

Jesus taught his followers not only how to serve but how to *be* served. Peter balked at Jesus wanting to wash his feet. He was willing to do the footwashing, but he wasn't willing to allow someone of Jesus' stature to wash his. Jesus demanded that we not only wash one another's feet, but let others scrub between our gnarly, dirty toes as well. Hospitality goes both ways, although I usually find it easier to wash the feet of others than to allow them to kneel and wash mine.

During dinner, Ma Li's mother urged me, "Chi, chi, chi"— "Eat, eat, eat." She plopped another lamb and cilantro dumpling into my bowl each time I emptied it. I never thought I'd resent someone's generosity the way I began to do that night. I felt bound by invisible rules that, as a Westerner, I didn't understand or recognize. In the United States, we urge our guests to "make yourselves at home" and "please help yourself." Our desire is that our visitors feel like members of the family. But in China and most non-Western cultures, hosts hope their guests feel like *guests*—special, honored, and set apart from the rest of the family.

Permitting my hosts to serve me somehow tipped the power scales to them. In *Cross-Cultural Servanthood*, Duane Elmer says, "We sometimes honor others most by receiving their kindness and hospitality and music rather than by trying to give to them."[2] By yielding our power and submitting, we can amplify the dignity of our host. Could it be that as we drop down in humility, our hosts rise in honor?

After dinner, Ma Li carried mandarin oranges, roasted chestnuts, and walnuts to the table. Family members and neighbors trickled in to peek at me, the foreigner, and I tried not to let the unsolicited attention bother me.

When the windows drew in darkness and cold numbed our noses, we played cards with Ma Li's siblings on the *kang*, our laps draped with musty blankets. I pretended I already knew how to play *Sheng ji*, a complicated game that seemed to be a combination of Hearts, Spades, and Rook. A single fluorescent bulb dangled from the ceiling, illuminating the black, white, and red playing cards. The cards were a comforting universal in a country of question marks.

At midnight, my two students, Ma Li's mother, and I all nestled under the weighted comforter, the heat of our bodies compounding while the flame within the *kang* lapped at us from below. I awoke stiff from the cardboard-lined concrete bed. My body odor was tinged with the smell of burnt manure, a scent that jumped into my personal repertoire of familiar smells, forever signaling the Chinese countryside to me.

Two days later, I relied on my students to choose when to travel back to our university, although internally I wrestled and thrashed, longing to decide for myself. After two nights of being served, fussed over, stared at, laughed at, and deemed a "genius" because of my talent for using chopsticks (though I had lived in China six months), I yearned to return home to my quiet cinderblock apartment where I could sauté my own spinach, watch *Alias* in English, and maintain full control of my time. As an independent and capable person, I was finding that leaning on others twisted my comfort and control into peculiar contortions.

When we're used to leading, following lacerates our pride and reveals our impulse to be in charge. Experiences like these agitated my Western guest-host assumptions, exposing my preference for serving over being served. I discovered that serving others stoked my own sense of power and worth. I preferred to be needed over being in need. But bowing to the discipline of discomfort and receiving hospitality is often the best spiritual practice for learning selfless love. If we can't accept the kindness of others, how can we expect to receive from God? If we can't stroll the fields as a sheep, how can we accept our need for a shepherd?

It's difficult to tap-dance to the tempo of another family's metronome—no matter the country. But sometimes the unexpected disturbance of the regular flow is a welcome syncopation to our rhythm of life.

* * *

Many of us in the West hate owing anyone anything. We extract ourselves from financial obligations to our parents as soon as possible. We don't expect handouts, scurry to pay back debts (hopefully), and loathe asking for help. This plays out in Colorado when friends stop by our home on their way up to Rocky Mountain National Park in the summertime and reserve a hotel rather than inconvenience us, even though I beg them to stay. Others reluctantly agree to sleep over, but supply their own towels, cornflakes, and pillows. What our guests don't realize is that in not accepting our gifts, they deny *us* the joy of giving.

In China, a cultural concept called *guanxi* describes how relationships are intentionally kept imbalanced. When someone asks you out to eat, they pay for you, and the unspoken rule is that you will invite them the next time. They rarely say thank you, because this reimburses the favor instead of leaving the tab open. Keeping an uneven balance in giving and receiving fuses us in ways that challenge our culture's insistence on individualism and independence.

Sometimes, for the sake of relationship, we ask for help even when we're capable of helping ourselves. In China, I often had students take me shopping or teach me to cook, when by my third year, I knew perfectly well where I could buy a step stool or how to fry eggs and tomatoes. But by helping, my students and colleagues felt useful, honored, and valued, and I savored their companionship. I've discovered the same thing in marriage—yes, I could try to do every household chore by myself, but by allowing my husband to participate, I remember we're bonded in a domestic partnership of mutual footwashing. Need is often the glue of relationship.

So much about being new homeowners puzzled us when we first bought our house in Colorado. Although Google offered answers on how to care for our lawn and clean our gutters, we found that depending on our neighbors positioned us in a posture of need. Asking them how to fix a sprinkler head or battle bindweed, or borrowing their extension ladder, shop vac, or saber saw indebted us to them. The relationship tab was left open and unbalanced—and we hoped they'd eventually call in the favor. Even Jesus, who could have filled his purse and belly with a word, often relied on the generosity of others to support his ministry. Jesus wasn't only a guest at his birth, but in his adulthood as well. In fact, Jesus was a guest more often than he was a host.

* * *

Jesus was a guest in the homes of Mary, Martha, and Lazarus; Zacchaeus; Simon; Levi; the men he met on the road to Emmaus; tax collectors; sinners; Pharisees; and many others. Matthew 8:20 says that Jesus didn't have a place to lay his head. In the book of John, the first recorded miracle of Jesus takes place at a wedding where he was a guest.

Why would Jesus, who had supernatural power at his disposal, intentionally put himself in a position of weakness and lack? Why would the Savior of the world position himself as a guest when he could have spoken seed and water, shirt and shelter into existence?

I can only guess. But perhaps it was because Jesus knew humans created in the image of God intuitively yearn to help one another. Maybe Jesus recognized that open palms invite intimacy.

Jesus often invited himself over, setting the precedent that sometimes we, too, need to ask ourselves into another person's life. Our Saudi friend Norah, the graduate student who lived with us for a year in Chicago, often invited herself along on many of our adventures. As Westerners, Adam and I tended toward privacy and the bubble of our nuclear family. Because Norah was so capable, sometimes it didn't occur to us to invite her along on activities like camping, road trips south for Thanksgiving, or traveling to visit family. But when she asked if she could join us, we never said no. Our children's memories now include Auntie Boo sliding off the air mattress while sleeping in a tent on her first camping trip, sitting with the kids on the sixteen-hour drive from Chicago to Winder, Georgia, for Thanksgiving on the farm, and staying in their grandma's home in Dixon, Illinois. And because she boldly invited herself along, Auntie Boo became like family.

* * *

I recently stumbled across a Bible story I hadn't noticed before. A widow was about to starve, and a prophet named Elisha asked what she had in her home. "A jar of olive oil," she replied.

"Go around and ask all your neighbors for empty jars. Don't ask for just a few," he told her.

When she poured olive oil from her jar into the other containers, she filled every single one (2 Kings 4:1-7). In faith, she offered what she had—much like the little boy in the miracle of Jesus feeding the five thousand. But she also depended on the community to provide for her, even if just to offer her an empty vessel. If we practice hospitality alone, we quickly burn out. If we give away our last vessel to our guests, we don't have anything left to refill. But when we rely on help from others, our flames flicker longer, higher, and hotter than if we tried to survive on our own.

Sometimes we're so depleted that practicing hospitality would drain the last dregs of our reserves. My friend Liz and her husband both have jobs working with people in trauma, so their home is a refuge for refueling. Maybe we have a new baby, an illness, or are tangled in work commitments. The reservoir is dry. But if the church is functioning in a healthy way, those who are full *should* supply the needs of the empty (2 Corinthians 8:14). Emptiness isn't always a sign that we should stop inviting; it often just means we need to call in reinforcements.

The month before we moved out of our rental and into our new home in Colorado, I asked five friends from various churches we had visited to help paint the main room. We turned up the music, poured silky paint into pans, and grabbed rollers and brushes. Ana edged the ceiling, Jess detailed the space between cabinets and counters in my kitchen, Shelby and Julie covered swaths of wall with rollers, and Liz knelt to paint the trim in thick, white paint.

Delivering drinks and checking in with each friend, I internally struggled to relinquish control when they painted in ways I wouldn't have. Days later, I rubbed fine steel wool over the many drips my friends had splattered on the oak floor. But for months afterward, when I gazed at the edging along the ceiling, the detail above the toaster, the gray walls, and the alabaster trim, I thought of the person each part represented.

Families and individuals who serve without the web of a wider community quickly fizzle out. Several friends of mine who are the parents of foster children have complained about the lack of support from the church. My friend Katie, a foster mom, writes that "the body of Christ has a responsibility to be the village to foster families. Not everyone is called to be on the front line, but everyone can do something and rally around a family for the long term."[3] Perhaps if foster families had more meals, babysitters, eyes, ears, and hands to hold little ones, they wouldn't fade so quickly. Like the women and midwives surrounding Mary at the birth of Jesus, perhaps we embrace the role of midwife and birth attendant, coming alongside others as they birth mystery and might into the world. Other times, we are Mary, begging for hands to help us. Receiving hospitality rams us up against our walls of self-sufficiency, especially when God uses not friends or family, churches or small groups, but total strangers to topple them.

* * *

Two deer wandered onto Interstate 80 somewhere between Des Moines and Iowa City in the deep black of predawn. The kids slept in pretzel formations, and Adam reclined in the passenger seat beside me on our drive from Colorado to Illinois to visit his mom for Thanksgiving. Hurtling seventy-five miles per hour on cruise control, I plowed into the first doe before my foot found the brakes. Sickened, I thought we were dragging her from the frame of our minivan, an object scraping the ground. I slowed to a stop on the narrow strip of shoulder, a single swirl of smoke from the hood curling up-ward into the starry night. The kids wailed and Adam stared at me in groggy stupefaction: What just happened?

Our parked minivan swayed violently with each eighteen-wheeler that barreled past us, and I fumbled to switch on the hazards so drivers would spy us in the dark. The hazards mal-functioned, so I turned on two inside lights instead. Some trucks, careening around the curve, shifted to the passing lane at the last moment. Others, not spotting us at all, swept within feet of our darkness-shrouded van, violently rocking us.

"It's going to be okay. We're going to be okay," I told our three panicking, pajama-clad kids, hoping it was true. I waited for a pause in the blinding headlights behind us before opening my door. It wouldn't budge, so Adam hopped out to assess the damage. The entire left side of the hood was gone, leaving the innards of the car spilling out and exposing a tangle of wiring. The only evidence of the deer was a tuft of blond hair on the inner fender, now bent into the rubber.

Roadside assistance from our insurance company alerted the police, called a rental company, and deployed a tow truck. After an hour of anxious waiting, two police officers arrived to shuttle us in their cars to the doorstep of a Perkins restaurant. "Here's my personal cell number if you need anything," one of them said to Adam, handing him a business card with a number written in pen. We stumbled into Perkins, frazzled and bedraggled after driving ten hours through the night.

"We hit a deer," I told the hostess, to explain our shabby appearance. "Would it be okay if we hung out here for a little while? We're hungry and don't mind buying food."

"Oh, you poor things," she said, leading us back to a table. "Of course it's okay. Come have a seat. Would you like some coffee, hon?"

"I'd love some," I answered, situating the kids on the vinyl booth and sliding in after them.

Adam spent the next hour on the phone while I ordered pancakes and bacon, corralling the bouncy, squawking kids in the booth and wiping their sticky fingers with napkins. A couple came over to our table and introduced themselves.

"We wondered if we could help you somehow," the woman said.

"Yeah, we heard you need to get to Des Moines to pick up a rental car. We're heading there soon. Would your husband like a ride?" the man asked.

The woman offered to bring the kids and me back to her home. "I have tons of toys there for my grandkids," she said.

"Oh, thank you, I think we'll be fine here for a little while longer," I said. "But we might take you up on that ride."

The Perkins staff allowed us to pile our suitcases, sleeping bags, and stuffed animals into two booths at the back of the restaurant. The tow truck had hauled our minivan over from the interstate, stopping briefly at Perkins for us to retrieve our things before it made its way to the auto repair shop. Adam left with the two strangers to pick up the rental car, and I set up our tablet for the kids to watch *Sesame Street*. I ordered another carafe of coffee and slid into the booth behind them. Digging my journal out of a bag, I sorted jumbled thoughts into neater categories and only then began to absorb the horrors of a "what if?" conclusion to the story.

On the ride to the restaurant, the police officer had told me they'd recently lost several officers to accidents with deer along that stretch of road. In one case, the deer had catapulted over the hood into the windshield, leaving the driver with a disability and brain damage. I shuddered as I considered alternative outcomes to our deer encounter.

Another man and woman approached my table and I looked up. "We heard what happened," the woman said, smoothing her white hair and pulling out a tissue to wipe her eyes. "Is there anything we can do?" she asked, sniffing. We chatted for a little while, and I assured them we were being taken care of. We were okay. Shaken, but okay.

After they left, I peered out the window, thinking about the hospitality of strangers. The week before, Adam and I had attended a touring Broadway show in Denver called *Come from Away*, about the thirty-eight planes diverted to Gander,

Newfoundland, on September 11, 2001. On a much smaller scale, I related to the stranded passengers utterly dependent on the kindness of others. In his book about the hospitality in Gander, author Jim DeFede wrote that "if the terrorists had hoped their attacks would reveal the weaknesses in Western society, the events in Gander proved its strength."[4]

Although we spent just a few hours adrift, displaced passengers in Canada spent up to six days in homes, churches, schools, and other public buildings. Gander, population ten thousand, welcomed over six thousand strangers from one hundred countries. The musical celebrated the hospitality lavished on scared travelers forced to wait out the tragedy in a strange town.

Sebastian Junger, the author of *Tribe*, found that people who have gone through trauma and tragedy together later miss the social bond created by those trying times. He writes that "twenty years after the end of the siege of Sarajevo, I returned to find people talking a little sheepishly about how much they longed for those days. More precisely, they longed for *who they'd been* back then."[5] Those in Gander also reunited years after the tragedy, as some had forged lifelong friendships. Helping people, living for others, and meeting a need feels good—it forces us to become better people. Junger notes, "Humans are so strongly wired to help one another—and enjoy such enormous social benefits from doing so—that people regularly risk their lives for complete strangers."[6]

Adam finally returned hours later with a rental car. I handed the kids their sleeping bags to carry outside to Adam, who was packing the car. I wheeled our oversized suitcase over the carpeted restaurant floor when another man stopped me. "Do you guys need a ride?" he asked. "If you're walking, I don't mind giving you all a lift somewhere."

"Thanks so much," I answered. "We have a rental car now. But thank you."

I marveled at the hospitality of strangers toward our stranded family at a Perkins restaurant in Iowa. Their kindness reminded me of the angels sent to minister to Jesus after he spent forty days fasting in the desert, to Elijah as he lay exhausted in the wilderness, and to Hagar when she was stranded in the desert with her son. Sometimes, as in the case of Abraham and Sarah, we entertain heavenly beings—maybe without even realizing it. Other times, God deploys plainclothes angels to welcome and rain hospitality on us as a reminder that we are not forgotten.

I snapped a picture of the Perkins sign and storefront before hoisting myself into the rental car, although I knew I wouldn't need the reminder. "You know," Adam said, easing back onto the interstate as the kids drifted off to sleep, "they didn't even let us pay for our meal."

Hospitality is one form of worship.

—Jewish proverb

TEN

A Shared Life

For three years, I was forbidden to attend church. When I lived in China, my American-based organization didn't allow its six hundred English teachers to go to Chinese churches unless those churches were registered with the Communist government. The authorities sometimes cracked down on unregistered churches—called "underground churches" by many Westerners—and my organization wanted to protect us. They also hoped to prevent the underground churches from coming under scrutiny that could be brought on by conspicuous foreigners attending services.

Because our location was remote and we knew of few other foreign believers, my one teammate, Natalie, and I met on Sunday mornings, taking turns to plan our church "service." We listened to sermons online, read Bible passages aloud, and sang hymns along with a website that blared hymns on an organ in a key too high for both of us. While

I now sometimes cherish the simplicity of those days, at the time, I yearned for community.

One morning during my second year in China, I broke the "no underground church" rule. Mrs. Shu was like a mother to me during my years in China. Her eyes crinkled in all the places where smiles live, and she kept Natalie and me laughing with her questions and comments about our weird American ways. Her English name, Joy, fit her perfectly. She was involved in a local gathering of Christians and invited me to visit her unregistered church after I complained to her about feeling lonely. I hesitated, but agreed to go.

Mrs. Shu's church was located next to a brown trickle of a mostly dried-up river, made rancid by a factory dumping dairy products in the flow. A three-foot-tall crimson cross marked the not-very-secret-underground-church, so I knew exactly where to meet Mrs. Shu. On the morning of the illicit church visit, I put on my track pants and headband and pretended to go out for a run. As I approached the church, I ducked inside the rusty metal gate instead of continuing on my way. Surely attending church was a forgivable sin.

At the unregistered church, Mrs. Shu and I squeezed onto tiny benches with quilt covers stitched from a mish-mash of fabrics and patterns, the outsides of our thighs touching. The men perched on one side of the snug church building and the women on the other. The smell of the room reminded me of clothes pulled from the cedar trunk my parents kept in the attic of my childhood home. When we stood, the women lifted up on their tippy-toes to reach the too-high notes of the familiar hymns sung in Mandarin Chinese, "Holy, Holy, Holy," and "Joyful, Joyful, We Adore Thee." After the singing, an old man entered and preached an impassioned sermon, which I couldn't understand, but I nodded and smiled nonetheless.

Afterward, Mrs. Shu introduced me to her friends as if I were her own daughter. They welcomed me with grins, handshakes, and questions in their regional dialect, which Mrs. Shu slowly repeated in Mandarin for me. I understood so little, yet I sensed the presence of Jesus in their midst. I was finally among family in a country where I had felt like a stranger. The church members showed me hospitality, and at a great risk to themselves.

During my time in China, my Mandarin eventually evolved from stilted, awkward strums on a guitar to shifting fluidly from chord to chord without much thought or deliberation. By the time I left China, I read at a third-grade level, could write about one thousand Chinese characters, and could converse with friends in Chinese about loneliness and spirituality, fears and longings.

Before moving to China, I had admired missionaries like Hudson Taylor and Gladys Aylward, who adopted the dress, language, and customs of China. During my years in China, I tried to adapt to the culture as much as I could—studying Mandarin, watching movies in the language, and eating and cooking mainly Chinese food. I believed that if I became fluent enough, learned enough pop culture, or lived long enough in China, then I would finally be accepted.

I was wrong. I wasn't included in faculty meetings with other teachers or expected to do the same grunt work the Chinese teachers did. Students invited me out to dinner, men paid me special attention, and school leaders saved me the best seat in school assemblies and meetings. I secretly questioned whether people liked me—Leslie—or just my white American face. I began to realize that invitation doesn't always translate to welcome. Embedded in the Chinese language are the semantics of in-groups and out-groups. The word *China*, or *Zhong Guo*, means "Middle Country": the center of the world. The word for foreigner, *wai guo ren*, means "outside country person." By my fifth year in China, I knew the truth: no matter what I did, whom I knew, or what I learned, I would never belong. I would never be truly welcomed as family. I would always be an outsider.

The people I ultimately experienced kinship with in China were those like my Chinese friends Mrs. Shu and Hannah, with whom I shared a common faith in Jesus. The Spirit in us sometimes leaps when it recognizes the Spirit in another person, just as John the Baptist leaped within the womb of Elizabeth when Mary, a few months pregnant with Jesus, entered her home. In those moments, we connect despite language, cultural, and economic boundaries. My teammate Natalie and I called it "kingdom culture," though I'm sure we weren't the inventors of the phrase. It's the overlapping center in the Venn diagram of Western and Eastern Christian culture, the sphere shared by sons and daughters swaying to the same Spirit.

Jesus lived within the culture of his day, but he also operated outside it. He confounded the religious leaders and kept his own followers guessing. As he prayed for his disciples in John 17, Jesus said, "They are not of the world, even as I am not of it. Sanctify them by the truth; your word is truth. As you sent me into the world, I have sent them into the world" (vv. 16-18). Jesus and those of us who find our identity in him navigate the tension of living both inside and outside culture. Through Jesus, God edited the rules of belonging. In fact, God crafted a new culture and called it the kingdom. In that culture, we learn a new language of Love, translated best by the way we welcome.

* * *

My first year of teaching college students in China, I had passed around a sign-up sheet for groups of three students to come over on Sunday afternoons to teach me to cook Chinese food. When I made the announcement in class, the forty students had tittered excitedly.

But that particular night, I felt weary from functioning in another culture. Binge-watching television all evening seemed more appealing than hosting my students. The whole event usually took about four hours and extracted tons of emotional and mental energy as we struggled to communicate with their limited English and my baby Chinese language skills. I usually spent more than an hour afterward washing dishes alone by hand, as we would use every dish and pan in my kitchen. But that Sunday, although I nearly canceled, I decided to go ahead. I met Linda, Sunny, and Vivian at the school gate, and we linked elbows in pairs to walk the crowded, weeping willow–lined street to buy ingredients.

Sunny haggled with the vegetable vendor, insisting the prices were too high and demanding they lower the price from five cents to three. I handed over money after they reached a compromise, and she stuffed the leeks, cucumber, garlic, and ginger into a plastic bag, expertly twirling, twisting, and tying it. Next we ducked into the butcher shop and bought a quarter pound of steak.

We returned to my tiny kitchen and the students set to work. I watched over their shoulders, oil splattering the wall as the students bickered about how their mothers each made the dish differently. We eventually sat down to a feast, with steaming bowls piled high with homemade noodles and fresh vegetables. Fragrant garlic, onion, and ginger punctuated the air. I lit a candle, and we pulled up folding chairs to the coffee table where we ate.

At first, our conversation felt strained, with the students terrified of making mistakes in front of their foreign English teacher. Because of this, I had a box of prepared questions, which I often used to save us in the awkward silences such as this. I handed Vivian the box.

"Pick a question," I said.

She drew one and read it aloud: "If you could erase any word and meaning from the dictionary, what would it be?"

She thought for a minute, then answered, "Die."

I wasn't sure how to respond. "Why did you choose that word?" I finally said.

"My father died last month," she whispered, looking down at her hands as she spoke.

I told her I was sorry. I didn't know what else to say. But we each asked her a few questions about how she was coping before Sunny tactfully turned to Linda to ask about the question she had picked. Eating together and picking questions out of a silly box had pushed us from the surface down to the deeps. I thanked God I hadn't canceled.

After dinner, we walked over to a first-year party on campus. Usually, my nervous students refused to approach me or make small talk, but this time several girls rushed up to chat. As we spoke, I realized they had each been over to my home for a meal in the previous weeks. Their hands didn't shake, and they chattered and laughed more than my students usually did around me.

Ambling home alone in the cool shadows of the dorm buildings, I reflected on the difference a single meal had made in my relationships with my shy students. I remembered something I had read earlier that day by Brennan Manning in *The Ragamuffin Gospel*, and looked the quote up when I got home. "In the Near East, to share a meal with someone is a guarantee of peace, trust, fraternity, and forgiveness—the shared table symbolizes a shared life."[1] Simply sharing my table made these Chinese students feel comfortable sharing their lives with me. Our shared meal had eased open the window of relationship.

This concept of table sharing equating to life sharing doesn't just apply to Eastern cultures. God's plan all along was for us to sit around tables together, sharing stories and deepening our relationships with one another. Jesus himself consistently models this in the Bible. But in table fellowship, gathering, and hospitality we also experience the presence of God.

* * *

Bells chimed as Adam and I squeezed into the last pew of a drafty stone building for our first visit at Colorado Church Number Eighteen. Vintage stained glass windows depicted the parables of Jesus along the whitewashed walls inside the church. A young woman sang up front, accompanied by a bearded man striking a djembe drum with the heel of his hand. We followed along in the bulletin, singing hymns at a fast pace. We rose and sat, rose and sat, listened to the sermon, then rose and sat again.

As we bowed our heads for silent confession, I thought about the many churches we had visited. People were often quick to celebrate, praise, and dance in the aisles, but slow to lament, mourn, or confess their sins against one another. True hospitality requires listening, learning, lament, and repentance. I knew I wanted to attend a church that wasn't afraid to wade into these murky waters every once in a while.

When Paul, a Jewish man by religion, culture, and ethnicity, says, "For we were all baptized by one Spirit so as to form one body—whether Jews or Gentiles, slave or free—and we were all given the one Spirit to drink" (1 Corinthians 12:13), his conception of "body" is different from the scientific way we sever body and spirit in the West. In the West, our doctors diagnose us by examining the part that is hurting, not by assessing a seemingly healthy part. But most other non-Western cultures believe the human body makes the most sense when considered as a whole. Paul didn't bother convincing his readers of the interconnectedness of the body—as men and women from a Middle Eastern culture, they intuitively understood that. Paul stated, "If one part suffers, every part suffers with it; if one part is honored, every part rejoices with it" (1 Corinthians 12:26). If one part of the body of Christian community is injured—from abuse, rejection, loss, prejudice, addiction, or neglect—the whole body should ache.

After our time of silent confession at Church Number Eighteen, an usher dismissed us row by row to take communion. We crept forward in line, the wooden floor creaking with our steps. I assumed we would take communion as individuals. But as we reached the stage, the lines split off into two groups of about ten people on either side of the front of the church, with two church leaders inviting each group to stand in a huddle.

Adam and I followed the couple in front of us, and we waited in a circle facing inward. The pastor held out the already-broken loaf of bread, and I ripped off a piece as he said, "His body, broken for you, take and eat." He offered the bread to everyone in the group, and we each ate. Then he held out a circular brass tray with wine in the center cups and grape juice in the outer ones. "His blood, shed for you. Take and drink," he said. Taking a tiny cup of wine, I tipped it to my lips, the soft burn sliding down my throat into my insides. Adam and the others did the same.

"Is not the cup of thanksgiving for which we give thanks a participation in the blood of Christ?" Paul writes. "And is not the bread that we break a participation in the body of Christ? Because there is one loaf, we, who are many, are one body, for we all share the one loaf" (1 Corinthians 10:16-17). We declare our unity as one communal body in Jesus at what some congregations call the "love feast."

"Let's pray," the pastor said, and leaned in slightly, putting his palms on the back of the man and woman to his right and left. The rest of us in the group followed his lead and embraced until the circle closed in on itself.

People take communion in many ways: From the same chalice, wiped (or not wiped) clean by a priest with a cloth. From their seats as the tray is passed from person to person. From each other as they tear bread and dip it into a communal goblet. To me, receiving communion in a group this way felt the most like family sharing a table together.

For followers of Jesus, the communion table is the essence of divine hospitality. In communion, God is the host, the guest, *and* the meal. The Catholic Church often refers to communion, or the eucharist, as the host. God invites us to the table and enters into the face of every guest, and we consume the bread and wine offered as a reminder of the broken body and shed blood. Communion is an echo of when God invited Moses and Aaron and many other elders of Israel up to a mountain. Instead of striking them down for seeing God's face, "they saw God, and they ate and drank" (Exodus 24:11). The word *communion* in Greek is *koinonia*, meaning a family bond. Scholar Scott Hahn says that "with communion, we renew our bond with the eternal family, the family who is God, and with God's family on earth, the church."[2]

In the Old Testament, bread was a sign of God's covenant (Leviticus 24:5-9). In the New Testament, it is the sign of a new covenant of forgiveness through the death and resurrection of Jesus (Luke 22:19-20). While I often take this imagery of the broken body and poured-out blood of Jesus for granted, knowing about the Jewish customs and feasts adds depth to my experience of this sacrament. To a first-century Jew, bread and wine were a sign of divine presence. According to Brant Pitre, scholar of ancient Judaism, "the Hebrew word for the 'face' of God is *panim*, the same word used for the 'Bread of the Presence' or 'Bread of the Face' (Exodus 25:30). In other words, by showing the pilgrims the Bread of the *panim*, the priests in the Temple were fulfilling the Law that commanded that they 'see the Face' of the Lord."[3] Manna in the wilderness, the bread of the presence, and the Passover all point to Jesus as our daily bread, King eternal, and eternal feast.

Christians around the world use a variety of substances to represent the body and blood as they take communion: sweet potatoes and coconut milk in a village in Papua New Guinea; barley loaf and honey wine in Scotland; sugar cookies and pink lemonade in Myanmar; flatbread and grape juice in China; sticky rice and red Fanta in Thailand. In these countries, the variable is the type of substance, and the constant is the presence of God as believers share the communion table together.

In the final chapter of the book of Luke, two men encounter a stranger on the road from Jerusalem to Emmaus. As they discuss Jesus' death and rumors of his resurrection, the stranger storytells them through the arc of the Old Testament. He explains how every segment is a signpost in the maze of history, culminating in Jesus as the door to the kingdom. They urge the man to stay overnight with them, and he takes the role of host as he blesses the bread and hands it to them. Only then—in bread and wine, hospitality and togetherness—do they recognize Jesus for who he is. When he disappears in a puff, the men marvel, reflecting on how their chests had burned as they walked the dusty road with the vagabond Jesus. The breaking of bread triggered an awareness of Emmanuel, God with us—in their midst all along. In hospitality, they saw the face of God.

* * *

After we had been in our new house in Colorado for a year, a neighbor convinced me to plan a block party with her. The kids and I spent three afternoons knocking on neighbors' doors. We distributed crumpled-up flyers that, by the time my kids' sweaty hands gave them away, looked as if we had picked them up from the gutter. I discouraged the kids from climbing neighbors' fences, lawn sculptures, and decorative walls. I hollered at them when they jumped up to look in windows and shouted, "They're home! I can see the TV on!" and lectured them when they repeatedly mashed doorbells.

The day of the block party, foul weather edged us into my neighbor's garage, swept clean for the occasion. Adeline doted on a woman in a wheelchair, taking a bite of beef and offering her the other half. The neighbor, Vivian, laughed good-naturedly, assuring me she didn't mind. She had adopted eight children and had more than fifty foster kids in her home over a fifteen-year span. She was fluent in the language of children.

My neighbor Larissa, her husband, Mark, and their three kids walked up the driveway into the garage. They were attending the church we had been visiting for the past ten months where communion had felt like a feast with family. The previous Sunday, my kids had run wild through the sanctuary while I chatted with the children's director. I had asked her how I could help out, even if it was just holding babies on Sunday mornings. I doubt she knew the weight of my words, that they were far from flippant. What I *meant* was "I'm ready. We'll stay. We commit. Will you welcome us?" For now, *staying* feels like faithfulness.

Along with committing to a church, we're also seeking preexisting networks to dive into and submerge ourselves in the current of our city. Like the Israelites in exile, we're working toward and praying for its welfare. Now that Elijah has started kindergarten, I'm realizing how public school can serve as a hub in the wheel of a neighborhood. Many of us parents trek to school or pedal children in bike trailers, bumping up onto the sidewalk and leaning bikes full of little ones up against the fence. Two times a day, I mingle with other moms and dads who are equally mystified by parenting small strangers and ache for their children to find a friend on the playground. Secretly, I think we parents long for a friend too.

We've now observed our yard through all four seasons. In the spring, I had bought some plants as a grand gesture of Staying Put. As I dug holes, smashed the encased roots of potted plants, and dropped them into the dirt, I whispered over jasmine vines, star lilies, and purple hyssop, praying they would transfer from plant nursery to permanent home. I asked my neighbor across the street how to till this hard, dry soil and coerce it to receive my roots in the ground. Some plants barely survived, some died, but a few thrived, extending green branches to the sun and fragrant flowers to the rustling wind.

Recently, as I wandered to the garden on the side of the house, I noticed the twelve basil plants that Rahim, our Iranian friend, had given me in early July. They were tall and flowering. Thanks to him, we had enjoyed fresh pesto every week for much of the summer. Rahim had driven up with his family in a shiny new car just a few weeks earlier, unexpectedly dropping by to bring us an Iranian meal of spiced rice, carrots, and chicken. They shared the happy news—they had extended their visas and were enrolling the kids in school for another year. I hugged Azita and traded excited smiles with Rahim. My annual friends were becoming perennial ones.

At the block party, I watched as neighbors who had lived on the street for twenty-five years exchanged names for the first time. They chuckled at the fact they had never met, but agreed that busyness, family obligations, and work had insulated them in their homes. But they were there. They received an invitation to come, and they came, even if that space was an oil-stained garage with folding tables draped with plastic tablecloths. They just needed to be invited.

Epilogue

God uses the ordinary as symbols of the sacred: bread and wine, feasting and fasting, inviting and being invited. A meal equalizes, for as we dine together, we lift the same utensils to our lips and touch the same bread to our tongues. We join in a common ceremony uniting us as human beings by the primitive urge to eat and drink. And in our gathering, we sense the presence of God in our midst.

What if we always took Jesus' words about loving God and neighbor at face value? If we are called, chosen, and invited by God, then we call, choose, and invite. When it comes to hospitality, we don't hold out for ideal circumstances. As my mom always told me about having children, "You will *never* be ready." And there's never a perfect time to welcome. A simple invitation is often the most groundbreaking move we can make.

The more we search for ways to practically radiate God's love throughout the world, the more we discover the centrality of hospitality to God's plan for community. As hospitality becomes a resounding chorus in the rhythm of our regular lives, we find an increasing awareness of the preciousness of people and of God hidden in plain sight.

Invitation frames the entire love story of the Bible. In Genesis, God beckons Adam and Eve to savor the fruit in the garden of Eden (with a notable exception), and they revel in relationship with their Creator. And in the final book of the Bible, John scribbles down this compelling invitation: "The Spirit and the bride say, 'Come!' And let him who hears say, 'Come!' Let the one who is thirsty come; and let the one who wishes take the free gift of the water of life" (Revelation 22:17).

The rest of the Bible is flooded with the imagery of invitation. Abraham and Sarah invite supernatural visitors to eat with them. The child Samuel finally answers God who has been inviting him in the night, responding, "Here I am, Lord! Your servant is listening." Isaiah issues the classic invitation for the weary soul: "Come, all you who are thirsty, come to the waters; and you who have no money, come, buy and eat! Come, buy wine and milk without money and without cost" (Isaiah 55:1).

The New Testament sings of bread and wine, feasting and invitations: Jesus invites fishermen and tax collectors to follow him, turns water to wine at a wedding, prepares a forgiveness feast of fish on the beach, uses banquets as object lessons for loving as he loves, and invites his disciples to have their feet washed by him. In a divine paradox, Jesus both stands at the open door, inviting us to come inside, and knocks on the door of our greatest secrets, waiting to enter. Jesus urges us to hand over our heavy loads, saying, "Come to me, all you who are weary and burdened, and I will give you rest" (Matthew 11:28).

In one of the most intimate scenes in the New Testament, John reclines next to Jesus, leaning on his chest (John 13:23). This is acceptance, and belonging. This is invitation.

The entire Bible is an invitation to more relationship, more connection, more intimacy. I once thought special callings were reserved for the Christian elite—those who loved God "most"—but I have since discovered that more than being called to missions, full-time ministry, parenthood, teaching, surgery, counseling, accounting, writing, or any other job or vocation, our first calling is to intimacy with Jesus Christ. Jesus announces, "Here I am! I stand at the door and knock. If anyone hears my voice and opens the door, I will come in and eat with that person, and they with me" (Revelation 3:20). We are invited to hear him, invite him in, be with him, and eat with him. And out of the well of that love affair, we pour out love for one another.

We don't belong because we wear the right clothes, follow the right political party, speak the right lingo, or participate in the right sacraments and rituals of church life. We belong because Jesus invites us to approach the throne, devour the feast, bathe in his fountain, guzzle the living water, be filled to wholeness, and join in the community of the kingdom. We are chosen, accepted, and adored. We belong because we hold an invitation in our trembling hands with our name on it. We know the Host, and the Host delights in welcoming us.

We are invited.

And so we pray collectively, as one body:

Lord, pry the film from our eyes, the scales from our skin, the shield and sword from our hands. Equip us to notice the stranger and the strange. Embolden us to *be* the stranger and the strange. Pull us into the flow of your Spirit at work in the world, infusing our ordinary days with your extraordinary presence. Hold open our eyes to admire your wonders and delight in your mysteries. Fill us with gratitude for the paths you've paved for us, and all the ways you've proven that you are Emmanuel, God with us.

Motivate us to always invite, because you never stop inviting. Inspire us to welcome, because you lavish generosity on us and promise to refill the gifts we give away.

Come, Lord Jesus.

Let us live like invited ones.

Amen.

DISCUSSION AND REFLECTION QUESTIONS

CHAPTER 1: **The Quest for Community**

Scriptures to read: Jeremiah 29:4-14; Romans 12:9-16

1. When have you experienced community in your life?

2. What does ideal community look like to you?

3. Where do you find examples of individualism in your culture or church? Is this always negative? Why or why not?

4. Do you agree that "privacy can be the enemy to the open home"? In what way?

5. Discuss the advantages and disadvantages of technology when it comes to relationships.

6. How do you see evidence of loneliness in your own life and in society today?

7. How can you seek the welfare of the city or community where you live?

8. Share about a time when you moved. How long did it take you to feel at home? What helped with this transition?

CHAPTER 2: **Staying Put**

Scriptures to read: Luke 9:1-9, Acts 6:1-7

1. Are you a goer or a stayer? Give examples from your life.

2. Do you think there is an unspoken hierarchy or "cult of calling" in the church? Explain.

3. If you have stayed in one place for a long time, how can you grow even deeper roots where you live?

4. Do you think many people in the West have the "gift of mobility"? What are some of the repercussions of this?

5. How can you get more proximate to those on the margins of society? What sacrifices might you need to make to do this?

6. Why don't we ever need to do anything "sensational" for God to love us?

7. How does staying put influence our communities?

CHAPTER 3: **Stranger Love**

Scriptures to read: Luke 10:25-37; Matthew 25:31-46

1. If you were to draw a circle diagram like the author did, who would be in your different rings?

2. Can you give an example of a time when you were suspicious of a stranger who later became a friend?

3. Share an example of a time you felt invisible.

4. Who are the invisible people in your city or community?

5. What adjustments can you make to your life to start seeing, knowing, and loving strangers in your neighborhood and city or town?

6. Who is hardest for you to love? Who would you need to put in the blank for "Jesus is _____"?

7. Think about the right-next-to-you people. Who are they for you? Who is already on your Jericho road? How might God be calling you to get to know them better?

CHAPTER 4: **Linger Longer**
Scriptures to read: Matthew 18:1-5; John 4:4-26

1. Name three places in your city or town you'd like to visit. How could you be a tourist in your own city or community?

2. Share a time when you wandered or got lost somewhere and what you discovered.

3. How does the Spirit use nature and wonder as an invitation to a deeper relationship with God?

4. What are some ways you could be more "childlike"?

5. What would you need to say no to in order to reserve more time in your schedule to wander, linger, play, or drop in to visit a friend?

6. What is the correlation between love of people and love of place?

7. What are some questions you ask people to prompt the conversation to go deeper?

8. Do you agree that most Westerners are structured with their time? If so, how does this affect our relationships?

CHAPTER 5: **The Friendship Conundrum**

Scripture to read: 2 Corinthians 7:2

1. How do you make new friends?

2. Share about a season of life when you had a difficult time making new friends.

3. Do you find that you're more hesitant to make friends with people who are in transition? What is the value in doing this?

4. How have your friendships changed you?

5. How long would you say it takes to make a good friend?

6. How many friends are too many? Is there such a thing as "too many friends"?

7. How do you keep up with old friends and go deeper with new ones?

8. How does hospitality deepen our friendships?

CHAPTER 6: **Habits of Hospitality**

Scriptures to read: Romans 12:9-16; 1 Peter 4:7-11

1. What are your biggest hospitality hang-ups? Could you identify with any of the author's hesitations? Which ones?

2. How do meals together lead to deeper relationships?

3. If you could pick three hospitality ideas from this chapter (or from the list in the back of this book) of things to try, what would they be?

4. Have you ever done any of the ideas listed in this chapter? If so, share your experience.

5. How can you fit hospitality into your current season of life and context?

6. If you attend church, how could your church be more hospitable?

7. What do you already love to do? Who could you invite to join you?

CHAPTER 7: **Beyond Our Limits**
Scriptures to read: Luke 9:10-17; Acts 9:1-19

1. Share about a decision you made when fear was involved.

2. When has God taken you beyond your limits?

3. Is God "safe"? Why or why not?

4. What's the difference between fear and faith?

5. How do you make decisions about safety and risk? What do you consider as factors?

6. What would it mean for you to "scooch over a bit" to make room for Christ in your current season of life?

CHAPTER 8: **Solitude**
Scriptures to read: Matthew 14:13; John 15:5-8; Mark 3:7-10

1. What are some of the advantages and disadvantages of individualism when it comes to the spiritual life?

2. What is the connection between solitude and hospitality?

3. How can you find solitude in this season of your life?

4. Are you more extroverted or introverted? What are ways you can adapt hospitality to your personality?

5. How can introverts and extroverts balance out each other?

6. When should we take a break from practicing hospitality?

7. What kinds of boundaries do you need to have so you don't burn out from hospitality fatigue?

8. What are some spiritual practices you learned from this chapter?

CHAPTER 9: **Utterly Dependent**

Scriptures to read: Luke 2:1-21; 2 Kings 4:1-7

1. In your opinion, what is the hardest part about being a guest?

2. How does allowing ourselves to be served actually serve others?

3. What is the relationship between receiving from others and receiving from God?

4. What can we learn from being dependent on others? How is this the "glue" of relationship? (Do you agree with this statement?)

5. Do you find that it's easier for you to lead or follow? What can you learn from doing the opposite of what you're used to?

6. Who in your church or community can you come alongside to support?

7. Describe a time when you experienced lavish hospitality from a stranger.

CHAPTER 10: **A Shared Life**

Scriptures to read: John 17:13-18; Luke 24:13-35

1. If you are a follower of Jesus, how do you live both inside and outside your own culture?

2. When have you experienced God's presence as you met with other followers of Jesus?

3. Have you ever taken communion in another culture? Could you share about that experience?

4. How is God host, guest, and the bread? What are the implications of each of these roles?

5. How are you already sharing life with those in your neighborhood, city, and church?

6. How have you seen hospitality break down walls?

Epilogue

Scriptures to read: Revelation 22:17; John 13:23

1. How is the entire Bible a picture of divine hospitality?

2. What does it mean to live out our identities as "invited ones" in the world?

IDEAS FOR INVITING

This list offers ways to practice the principles of hospitality in different seasons and stages of life. It is less of a to-do list and more of a springboard to launch you into relationships within your own community and context. I hope these ideas prompt you to think outside the box and help broaden your hospitality horizons with your neighbors, church, community, overnight guests, friends, and soon-to-be friends. I also added a few ways we can include our children in our gatherings. At the end of this list, you'll find some general hospitality tips from this book as a reminder that hospitality doesn't need to be complicated or overwhelming. Please don't use this list as a way to berate yourself for what you are *not* doing. Instead, I hope you feel energized and inspired by all the unique ways we can enjoy our shared life together.

Neighbors

- Give new neighbors a gift basket to welcome them to the neighborhood.

- Intentionally spend time outside in your front yard or a public or other shared area. You may even want to put a picnic table or swing in your front yard.

- Go on walks in your neighborhood and talk to neighbors you meet. Ask some neighbors to regularly go on a walk with you.

- Invite neighbors to go with you to a local high school sporting event and have pizza afterward.

- Download the app Nextdoor to be informed about events in your neighborhood.

- Go sledding and invite neighbors back to your home for hot chocolate.

- Project a movie onto a garage door or external wall for an outdoor movie night. Or gather in your home to watch a televised sporting event, the Oscars, or a movie.

- Rotate soup nights in a different neighbor's home every week during winter months.

- Host a block party (many cities offer grant money for this).

- Organize a monthly cookout, taco night, soup night, pot-luck, campfire, or book club.

- Hold a garage or yard sale—and actually talk to the people who stop by.

- Host a cookie or soup exchange.

- Coordinate a clothing or stuff swap.

- Host a s'mores and campfire night in the fall or an ice cream social in the summer.

- Plan a neighborhood bike parade where kids decorate bikes beforehand. End with a barbecue.

- Invite neighbor kids for a kiddie pool and sprinkler hangout. Invite their parents to come over for a potluck or cookout.

- Organize your neighbors to help each other with yard work—helping earns you the privilege of receiving help for your yard.

- See if your neighbors might be interested in a neighborhood Easter egg hunt.

Get kids involved

- Have kids help you deliver invitations to neighbors for a party.

- Let your kids help you prepare the meal and set the table. Have them make place cards or small gifts for guests.

- If you have teenagers, tell them they are free to have their friends over to your home to hang out. (Hint: have lots of snacks.)

- Bake something to bring to a neighbor, and take it over together with your children.

- Ask your kids whom they would like to invite over for a meal. Consider inviting community members such as law enforcement, people on city council, or fire safety personnel.

- Get to know other parents at your kids' activities; invite the team to your home for a pre- or postgame or concert meal.

- Invite your kids' friends to join you on a hike or walk or at a park.

- Prioritize family dinners.

- Visit a nursing home with your kids.

- Help your kids set up a lemonade stand—introduce yourselves to the neighbors who stop by.

As a guest

- Bring a small gift to your host.

- If you're an overnight guest, leave a thank you note.

- Offer to help with meal prep or cleaning up afterward.

- Get your kids to clean up toys before you leave.

- Reciprocate and return the invite.

Church

- Invite a new family or person over to your home or out for lunch. (Maybe get a group together so individuals don't feel intimidated.)

- Invite a group of moms and their children over for coffee and muffins. Or host a weekly coffee group for parents of young children at your church.

- Have a new parents' brunch every quarter to encourage and support new parents.

- Have a weekly picnic or cookout after church during the summer.

- Accompany new visitors to the nursery, sanctuary, bathroom, or coffee area. Don't just point them in the right direction—walk with them. You may want to offer them your contact information.

- Display good signage and written information for church visitors.

- Invite college students, international students, single people, or widows or widowers after church—any time is wonderful, but especially during holidays.

- Invite your pastor or other church leader over to your home, or offer to bring them a meal on a Sunday.

- Host a newcomers' luncheon in a home or at your church.

- Invite one person or couple you want to get to know better over for lunch, tea, coffee, or dessert.

- Mark certain dates in the church calendar for celebration and invite a few people to join you.

- Even if you don't have young children, keep a few toys on hand for guests who may have kids.

- Pray for your neighbors and city in your church and Bible studies and pick a few ideas from the rest of this list to do together.

Community

- Learn the name of cashiers in the grocery store. Make eye contact, say thank you, and consider asking them questions about their day.

- Frequent the same parks, coffee shops, or library on the same days and times. Pay attention to who is there.

- Spend an extra five minutes talking to a stranger somewhere.

- Attend a local event—like a storytelling night at an independent bookstore, a town meeting, or a concert—and introduce yourself to someone. You could try the Meetup website for ideas that match your interests.

- Volunteer regularly at a nursing home, prison, ESL class, adult literacy class, school, homeless shelter, or pregnancy center. When appropriate, invite new friends back to your home.

- Find a program that helps refugee families adapt to life in your city.

- Invite your child's principal, coach, or teacher over for a meal.

- Invite parents and families from your child's school over for a party or cookout.

Overnight guests

- Open your home to foster children or be a Safe Family for children in transition.

- Become a host family for an international student through an exchange or service program.

- Invite a person coming out of prison or jail to live with you.

- If you have space, offer a room or rooms to a struggling family to live with you.

- Have your children share a room so you can have a guest room.

- Invest in a pull-out couch, air mattress, or futon.

Friends and soon-to-be friends

- Throw simple birthday parties for your kids and invite a wide variety of guests.

- Host a game night or an open-house-style game day.

- Cook a meal together with some people you want to get to know better.

- Invite those who love reading over for a "books and bottles party" where each person brings a favorite book and a bottle of something to drink to share. The host prepares book-related trivia and prizes as an opener. After that, each guest spends one minute introducing their book, then the guests exchange books "white elephant" style.

- Invite a group over for a "poetry, prose, and pour party" where each guest brings a drink and writing or art to share (if you do this with church friends, they could add a spiritual element).

- Host a music night where everyone brings an instrument and plays together.

- Plan a Valentine's Day party for married couples where each person brings an object to describe their spouse. The spouse has to guess what their partner might have brought and why. Play the Newlywed Game.

- Start a new tradition: weekly swing dance nights, Taco Tuesdays, or Friday night meatballs where you invite friends to bring salad, bread, and dessert.

- Offer to babysit a friend's kids or bring their kids along on your outings.

- Invite people into what you're already doing: sewing, watching a television show or game, making cards, freezer meal prep, baking, biking, hiking, jogging, cookie decorating, painting, or present wrapping.

- Ask coworkers over for dinner or dessert.

- Host a dinner with six to eight people. Ask each person to bring one course (this is a good opportunity to try some new recipes and non-kid-friendly food). Have questions prepared or a theme to discuss over your meal.

General tips for uncertain hosts

- If you have food, people will come.

- Ask your guests to bring something or to help you.

- Plan ahead, but don't be afraid to be spontaneous.

- Items to keep on hand if possible:

  - Disinfectant wipes to quickly clean the bathroom

  - Frozen food, such as cookies, banana bread, or lasagna, for last-minute hosting

  - Quick snacks like cheese and crackers, chips and salsa, apple slices, popcorn

- To combat decision fatigue, make the same meal every time. (My friend's parents made spaghetti every single Sunday and invited different families over after the church service.)

- Ask guests ahead of time if they have any food restrictions.

- Keep in mind that conversations can often go deeper with a smaller group.

- Prepare food in advance as much as possible.

- Invite someone to sit with you at church or a conference, retreat, or meeting.

- Remember that people are more significant than the environment, food, or cleanliness of the home.

- Hospitality doesn't have to happen inside your home.

- Go deep with a few, but also reach out to those who are not in the "friends or family" category—yet.

- Know that you are probably already doing more than you know in terms of hospitality.

- Remember that it's okay to take breaks for solitude to regroup and re-root yourself in the love of God.

- Don't forget: the more you practice hospitality, the easier it gets.

FURTHER READING

Community and relationships

Becoming Human, by Jean Vanier

Life Together: The Classic Exploration of Christian Community, by Dietrich Bonhoeffer

Living into Community: Cultivating Practices That Sustain Us, by Christine D. Pohl

One: Unity in a Divided World, by Deidra Riggs

Practicing the Presence of People: How We Learn to Love, by Mike Mason

Reaching Out: The Three Movements of the Spiritual Life, by Henri Nouwen

The Wisdom of Stability: Rooting Faith in a Mobile Culture, by Jonathan Wilson-Hartgrove

Cross-cultural considerations of the church and the Bible

Beyond Colorblind: Redeeming Our Ethnic Journey, by Sarah Shin

Disunity in Christ: Uncovering the Hidden Forces That Keep Us Apart, by Christena Cleveland

Jesus through Middle Eastern Eyes: Cultural Studies in the Gospels, by Kenneth E. Bailey

Lessons from the East: Finding the Future of Western Christianity in the Global Church, by Bob Roberts Jr.

Misreading Scripture with Western Eyes: Removing Cultural Blinders to Better Understand the Bible, by E. Randolph Richards and Brandon J. O'Brien

The Next Evangelicalism: Freeing the Church from Western Cultural Captivity, by Soong-Chan Rah

The Next Worship: Glorifying God in a Diverse World, by Sandra Maria Van Opstal

Sitting at the Feet of Rabbi Jesus: How the Jewishness of Jesus Can Transform Your Faith, by Ann Spangler and Lois Tverberg

Hospitality

The Art of Neighboring: Building Genuine Relationships Right Outside Your Door, by Jay Pathak and Dave Runyon

Just Open the Door: How One Invitation Can Change a Generation, by Jen Schmidt

Making Room: Recovering Hospitality as a Christian Tradition, by Christine D. Pohl

The Turquoise Table: Finding Community and Connection in Your Own Front Yard, by Kristin Schell

Wabi-Sabi Welcome, by Julie Pointer Adams

ACKNOWLEDGMENTS

Thank you to the team at Herald Press—especially to Valerie Weaver-Zercher for reaching out, believing in the concept behind this book, then pushing me to make it better. And to Melodie Davis and Sara Versluis, thank you for your attention to detail.

To the *SheLoves Magazine* editors and leadership team: Kathleen Bertrand, Leah Abraham, Claire Colvin, Holly Grantham, Chervelle Camille, Shaley Hoogendoorn, Annie Rim, and Claire de Boer. Knowing each of you has changed me at an elemental level. Thank you for your encouragement, support, and prayers. You helped me believe I could possibly write a book. Perhaps even a good one. And especially to Idelette McVicker, a woman of strength, compassion, and zeal: I am so honored to know you. I am grateful for the generosity, depth, and vulnerability you nurture within the SheLoves community.

To the beta readers for my proposal and manuscript: Afton Rorvik, Charlotte Donlon, Idelette McVicker, Amy Boucher Pye, Annie Rim, Amy Young, Michelle Reyes, Julene Barder, Megan Gahan, Nikki Wuu, Lisa Ohlen Harris, and Easten Law. Your feedback was the perfect balance of encouragement and critique.

Thank you for the hours you spent poring over my words. Nikki Wuu, I owe you free vanilla lattes for the rest of your life for the overtime you put into this project. To our little writing group that feels more like a support group: Annie Rim, Nicole Walters, Sheli Massie, and Megan Gahan, thank you for your friendship.

Real-life and virtual writer friends: Catherine McNiel, Alia Joy, Tammy Perlmutter, Kelley Nikondeha, Patrice Gopo, Ann Kroeker, Beth Bruno, Gena Thomas, and Ashley Hales. Thank you for letting me tweet, message, and vox you with my panicky questions. You loaned me books, cheered me on, and taught me what you know. Your generosity has brought me to tears on many occasions. Thank you for taking the time to guide me when I was still lost in this process.

The Inkwell writing group kept me grounded in what's real throughout this journey, reminding me to laugh when I mostly wanted to hyperventilate. To Tanya Marlow, I'm thankful for your wisdom, fire, graciousness, and thoughtfulness. To Abby Norman for telling me over and over again that I could do it. To Amy Boucher Pye for offering invaluable advice on my proposal and also for reading through an early draft. To Janice Andrews for your emotional and tech support. To Amy Young for understanding my "three-ness" and the third-culture undercurrent of my writing and life. Thank you for spending hours reading not only my proposal but also my first draft, and for giving the gift of encouragement at a time when I was mostly riddled with doubt.

Redbud Writers Guild has been a safe space to ask all manner of ridiculous questions. I discovered Redbud when I knew few writers, and many of these online relationships have become true friendships. Thank you for sharing your expertise, contacts, and insight with a new writer.

Fellow Herald Press authors Jenny Rae Armstrong, April Yamasaki, Sarah Quezada, Christiana Peterson, and Karen González did a lot of hand-holding along this road. Thank you. I'm honored to have my book nestled next to each of yours on book tables.

Dr. Scott Moreau at Wheaton College taught me most of what I know about cross-cultural communication and met with me to discuss this topic when my thoughts were still in the embryo stage. Your wisdom about crossing cultures rattled my world in the best of ways.

My friends in China, Uganda, and other countries I visited reframed hospitality for me. The international students who rented a room in our home expanded our worldview simply by sharing life with us. We now have friends in far-flung places because you took a risk by living with strangers. Thank you.

To our fabulous babysitter, Marsha, who watched my kids so I could sneak off to the library or lock myself in a room to tap away on my computer, I'm grateful. To the nuns at the Abbey of St. Walburga, who welcomed me as stranger to their sacred space and unknowingly taught me about stability, community, and liturgy.

To our new church home and Pastors Scott and Ryan; our small group who prayed me through revisions; and church friends who made me feel more stable in Fort Collins. After wandering so long, I am even more grateful for all of you.

Marie, Holly, Karen, Julene, Sarah, Brenda, Lizzy, Cami, the Esters, Kate, Shelley, Jen, and my other friends around the country: I'm grateful for women who know my layers. I have learned so much about having an open home from each of you.

To my Fort Collins neighbors for opening their garages, homes, and driveways, for welcoming my children to your backyards, and for responding to invitations from a weird new neighbor with a hankering for gathering strangers: I'm glad you are my village.

To my parents for modeling selfless hospitality my entire life. By welcoming people to live in our home, eat at our table, borrow our cars, and gather in our living room and kitchen, you taught me that home is not a place to protect. Home is a gift to share. Thank you for the ways you still take care of me, my kids, and even our guests when we visit. I love you and am so thankful to be just one snowy mountain range away from you.

To my "ancient mother" Nina, I am grateful for your encouragement, your strength, and your belief in me. (And thank *you* for raising such an incredible son.)

To my children for loving strangers, begging us to invite more people over, and reminding me our guests don't need a spotless floor or fancy meal. They just need an invitation. You teach me about lavish love. Thank you for sharing me with this book for the past year.

To my best friend and husband, Adam, who read this entire manuscript at least five times. The only reason this book exists is because you believed, coached, and prayed me into doing this. Countless times, you took me by the shoulders, looked into my eyes, and said, "You *can* do this." You encouraged me to take the next step, and then the step after that. And here we are. Your constant prayers have fueled any power within these pages. I would never have had the audacity to call myself a writer if it weren't for you. Thank you for picking up my slack, believing in me, loving me, and urging me to serve the work.

And to Jesus for all the tiny invitations that remind us we are so loved, so wanted, so adored. I'm grateful for a God with wide arms who chooses welcome.

NOTES

Epigraph

Jane Kenyon, "Briefly It Enters, and Briefly Speaks," in *Otherwise: New and Selected Poems* (Saint Paul: Greywolf Press, 1996), 115.

Chapter 1: The Quest for Community

1. Chrissy Esposito, "Suicides in Colorado: 2017 Trends," updated September 12, 2018, https://www.coloradohealthinstitute.org/research/suicides-colorado-reach-all-time-high.

2. Jim Silwa, "So Lonely I Could Die," American Psychological Association, August 5, 2017, www.apa.org/news/press/releases/2017/08/lonely-die.aspx.

3. G. Oscar Anderson and Colette Thayer, "Loneliness and Social Connections: A National Survey of Adults 45 and Older," AARP Research, September 2018, https://www.aarp.org/research/topics/life/info-2018/loneliness-social-connections.html.

4. Ceylan Yeginsu, "Britain Tackles Loneliness," *New York Times*, January 18, 2018, A7.

5. Susan Pinker, *The Village Effect: How Face-to-Face Contact Can Make Us Healthier, Happier, and Smarter* (New York: Random House, 2014), 61.

6. Soong-Chan Rah, *The Next Evangelicalism: Freeing the Church from Western Cultural Captivity* (Downers Grove, IL: IVP Books, 2009), 30.

7. E. Randolph Richards and Brandon J. O'Brien, *Misreading Scripture with Western Eyes: Removing Cultural Blinders to Better Understand the Bible* (Downers Grove, IL: IVP Books, 2012), 108. The authors mention this phenomenon, pointing out that "a flaw in the English language works together with our love for individualism. In English, you can be both singular and plural. That is, we can't differentiate formally between *you* (singular) and *you* (plural). . . . Biblical Greek could differentiate between *you* singular and *you* plural. But we miss this in our English translations. Paul asked the Corinthians: 'Do you not know that your bodies are temples of the Holy Spirit, who is in you, whom you have received from God? You are not your own' (1 Corinthians 6:19). We typically understand the singulars and plurals in this verse backwards. In the original Greek, the *you* is plural and *temple* is singular. Paul is saying, 'All of you *together* are a *singular* temple for the Holy Spirit.' God doesn't have millions of little temples scattered around. Together we make the dwelling for the Spirit." Ibid.

8. Philip Slater, *The Pursuit of Loneliness: American Culture at the Breaking Point* (Boston: Beacon Press, 1976), 33.

9. Ibid., 13.

10. Geert Hofstede and Gert Jan Hofstede, *Cultures and Organizations: Software of the Mind* (New York: McGraw-Hill, 2005), 79.

11. Jean M. Twenge, "Has the Smartphone Destroyed a Generation?," *The Atlantic*, September 2017, https://www.theatlantic.com/magazine/archive/2017/09/has-the-smartphone-destroyed-a-generation/534198/.

12. Grace H. Kim, "How Co-housing Can Make Us Happier (and Live Longer)," filmed April 2017 in Vancouver, BC, TED video, 10:16, https://www.ted.com/talks/grace_kim_how_cohousing_can_make_us_happier_and_live_longer.

Chapter 2: Staying Put

1. Thomas Merton, *The Sign of Jonas* (San Diego: Harcourt, 1981), 10.

2. Jonathan Wilson-Hartgrove, *The Wisdom of Stability: Rooting Faith in a Mobile Culture* (Brewster, MA: Paraclete Press, 2010), 19.

3. Mark Labberton, "Wayne Gordon on Community," January 10, 2017, in *Conversing*, podcast, MP3 audio, 43:39, http://conversing .libsyn.com/5-wayne-gordon-on-community.

4. Bryan Stevenson, "An Evening with Bryan Stevenson" (author series talk, Colorado State University, Fort Collins, CO, September 22, 2016).

5. Michelle Warren, *The Power of Proximity: Moving beyond Awareness to Action* (Downers Grove: IVP Books, 2017).

6. Ibid., 120.

7. John Perkins, *A Quiet Revolution: The Christian Response to Human Need, a Strategy for Today* (Waco, TX: Word Books, 1976), 213–16.

8. Morgan Neville, dir., *Won't You Be My Neighbor?* (Los Angeles: Tremolo Productions, 2018).

9. Paul Tillich, *The New Being* (New York: Charles Scribner's Sons, 1955), 46–49.

10. Jessica Alexander and Iben Sandahl, *The Danish Way of Parenting: A Guide to Raising the Happiest Children in the World* (Copenhagen: Ehrhorn Hummerston, 2014).

Chapter 3: Stranger Love

1. "Get Involved," International Students, Inc., accessed February 18, 2019, https://www.isionline.org/GetInvolved.aspx.

2. In fact, the Samaritan "risks his life by transporting the wounded man to an inn within Jewish territory. . . . A Samaritan would not be safe in a Jewish town with a wounded Jew over the back of his riding animal. Community vengeance may be enacted against the Samaritan, even if he has saved the life of the Jew." Kenneth E. Bailey, *Jesus through Middle Eastern Eyes* (Downers Grove: IVP Academic, 2008), 295.

3. Jay Pathak and Dave Runyon, *The Art of Neighboring: Building Genuine Relationships Right outside Your Door* (Grand Rapids: Baker Books, 2012), 38.

4. Sally Lloyd-Jones, *The Jesus Storybook Bible* (Grand Rapids: Zondervan, 2007), 26.

5. Dorothy Day, *Dorothy Day: Selected Writings: By Little and by Little*, ed. Robert Ellsberg (New York: Orbis Books, 1992), 94.

6. Ibid., 97.

7. Ibid., 291.

Chapter 4: Linger Longer

1. Brenda Ueland, *If You Want to Write . . .* (Mansfield Centre, CT: Martino, 2011), 32.

2. Luci Shaw, *Breath for the Bones: Art, Imagination, and Spirit: Reflections on Creativity and Faith* (Nashville: Thomas Nelson, 2007), 87.

3. William Shakespeare, "Sonnet 29" in *Shakespeare's Sonnets*, ed. Edward Bliss Reed (New Haven: Yale University Press, 1965), 15, lines 11–12.

4. Mike Mason, *Practicing the Presence of People: How We Learn to Love* (Colorado Springs: Waterbrook Press, 1999).

5. Ibid., 269, 270.

6. Susan Pinker, *The Village Effect: How Face-to-Face Contact Can Make Us Healthier, Happier, and Smarter* (New York: Random House, 2014), 7–8.

7. Ibid., 65.

8. G. Oscar Anderson and Colette Thayer, "Loneliness and Social Connections: A National Survey of Adults 45 and Older," AARP Research, September 2018, https://www.aarp.org/research/topics/life/info-2018/loneliness-social-connections.html.

9. Barbara Brown Taylor, *An Altar in the World: A Geography of Faith* (New York: Harper One, 2009), 33.

Chapter 5: The Friendship Conundrum

1. Anne Morrow Lindbergh, *Gift from the Sea* (New York: Random House, 2005), 20.

2. Malcolm Gladwell, *The Tipping Point: How Little Things Can Make a Big Difference* (New York: Hachette Book Group, 2002), 177.

3. Ibid., 180.

4. Dee Brestin, *The Friendships of Women: The Beauty and Power of God's Plan for Us* (Colorado Springs: Cook, 2008).

5. Carl Jung, *Modern Man in Search of a Soul* (New York: Harcourt, Brace and Company, 1933), 57.

Chapter 6: Habits of Hospitality

1. Kristin Schell, *The Turquoise Table: Finding Community and Connection in Your Own Front Yard* (Nashville: Thomas Nelson, 2017).

2. Beth Bruno, "Interview with Tracy Johnson," September 18, 2018, in Fierce and Lovely, podcast, MP3 audio, 52:36, https://fierceandlovelypodcast.simplecast.fm/episode2.

3. Alexander Strauch, *The Hospitality Commands: Building Loving Christian Community: Building Bridges to Friends and Neighbors* (Littleton, CO: Lewis and Roth, 1993), 18.

4. Mike and Sally Breen, *Family on Mission: Integrating Discipleship into the Fabric of Our Everyday Lives*, 2nd ed. (Greenville: 3DM, 2018).

5. Jay Pathak and Dave Runyon, *The Art of Neighboring: Building Genuine Relationships Right Outside Your Door* (Grand Rapids: Baker Books, 2012).

6. Rosaria Butterfield, *The Gospel Comes with a House Key: Practicing Radically Ordinary Hospitality in Our Post-Christian World* (Wheaton: Crossway, 2018).

7. D. L. Mayfield, *Assimilate or Go Home: Notes from a Failed Missionary on Rediscovering Faith* (New York: Harper One, 2016).

8. Shannan Martin, "This Is What It Feels Like to Talk to the Wind," *Shannan Martin Writes* (blog), March 6, 2018, http://www.shannanmartinwrites.com/2018/03/this-is-what-it-feels-like-to-talk-to.html.

9. Kelley Nikondeha, *Adopted: The Sacrament of Belonging in a Fractured World* (Grand Rapids: Eerdmans, 2017), 66.

10. See Safe Families For Children, https://safe-families.org/.

Chapter 7: Beyond Our Limits

1. C. S. Lewis, *The Lion, the Witch, and the Wardrobe* (New York: Scholastic, 2006), 80.

2. Erwin W. Lutzer, *When a Nation Forgets God: 7 Lessons We Must Learn from Nazi Germany* (Chicago: Moody Press, 2010), 22.

3. David P. Gushee, *Righteous Gentiles of the Holocaust: Genocide and Moral Obligation* (Saint Paul: Paragon House, 2003), 79.

4. Corrie ten Boom, *The Hiding Place* (New York: Bantam Books, 1971), 99.

5. Linda Ashman (author) and Chuck Groenink (illus.), *William's Winter Nap* (New York: Disney Books, 2017).

6. Shel Silverstein, *The Giving Tree* (New York: Harper and Row, 1964).

7. Christine D. Pohl, *Making Room: Recovering Hospitality as a Christian Tradition* (Grand Rapids: Eerdmans , 1999), 45.

Chapter 8: Solitude

1. Mary F. C. Pratt, "Not like a Dove," in *Still Point*, ed. Sarah Arthur (Massachusetts: Paraclete Press, 2011), 18.

2. Sandy Dengler, *Susanna Wesley: Servant of God* (Chicago: Moody Publishers, 1987).

3. Arnold Lobel, "Alone," in *Frog and Toad: Storybook Treasury* (New York: Harper Collins, 2014), 242–54.

4. Quoted in Robert Coles, *Dorothy Day: A Radical Devotion* (Massachusetts: Perseus Books, 1987), 130–31.

5. Henri Nouwen, *Reaching Out: The Three Movements of the Spiritual Life* (London: Fount, 1998), 56.

6. Thomas Merton, *Seeds of Contemplation* (New York: Dell Publishing House, 1948), 51.

Chapter 9: Utterly Dependent

1. Kenneth Bailey, *Jesus through Middle Eastern Eyes: Cultural Studies in the Gospels* (Downers Grove: IVP Academic, 2008), 34.

2. Duane Elmer, *Cross-Cultural Servanthood: Serving the World in Christlike Humility* (Downers Grove: IVP Books, 2006), 47.

3. Katie Finklea, "What I Wish a Friend Would Have Told Me over Coffee about Foster Care," *Scraping Raisins* (blog), May 7, 2018, http://www.scrapingraisins.com/2018/05/what-i-wish-a-friend -would-have-told-me-over-coffee-about-foster-care-guest-post/.

4. Jim DeFede, *The Day the World Came to Town: 9/11 in Gander, Newfoundland* (New York: Harper, 2002), 7.

5. Sebastian Junger, *Tribe: On Homecoming and Belonging* (New York: Twelve, 2016), 66–67.

6. Ibid., 55.

Chapter 10: A Shared Life

1. Brennan Manning, *The Ragamuffin Gospel* (Colorado Springs: Multnomah Publishers, 1990), 59.

2. Scott Hahn, *The Lamb's Supper: The Mass as Heaven on Earth* (New York: Doubleday, 1999), 56.

3. Brant Pitre, *Jesus and the Jewish Roots of the Eucharist: Unlocking the Secrets of the Last Supper* (New York: Doubleday, 2011), 132.

THE AUTHOR

Leslie Verner writes about faith, justice, family, and cross-cultural issues for *SheLoves*, *Relevant*, *The Mudroom*, and other venues. She earned her master's degree in intercultural studies and bachelor's in elementary and middle grade education at Wheaton College. She lived in China for five years, where she taught English as a second language and studied Mandarin. Verner, her husband, and their three children live at the foothills of the Rocky Mountains in Colorado. Verner is a member of the Redbud Writers Guild. Connect with her at www.scrapingraisins.com.

CPSIA information can be obtained
at www.ICGtesting.com
Printed in the USA
LVHW110017180719
624476LV00003B/40/P

9 781513 804347